Praise for *How to Succeed with Continuous Improvement*

"I love it! This book is exceedingly well written. The writing style is perfect for revealing insights and lessons learned from a lean journey. I like the reflections at the end—a nice way to share overall lessons learned. The use of language and examples of lean (with supporting illustrations) are very well done. People new to the lean journey will feel empowered with the simplicity of these concepts. This book deserves a big audience!"

—Mike Morrison
Founder of the University of Toyota

"This book is more than inspiration on your journey to implement continuous improvement. It also gives you valuable methods that can easily be applied and understood by everyone. It is the most valuable and lean book I have read about lean and will help any organization to become the best in the world."

—Göran Martinsson
Continuous Improvement Manager
IKEA

"Using a story he lived through, Joakim vividly brings to life for us the transformation from a mediocre top-down organization depending on a few internal experts for its survival to a high-performance organization of empowered employees engaged in continuous improvement."

—Jeffrey Liker
Bestselling author of *The Toyota Way*

"Everyone who wants to improve should read and keep this book on their desktop. It is entertaining and shows that it does not have to be difficult to create an improvement culture. I should warn you, though, when you are done reading it you will not be able to think of anything else than your next improvement project."

—Patrik Färdow
CEO
G4S Cash Solutions Sweden

"Follow Joakim's recommendations, simplicity is key, do your improvement work this way to deliver world-class results. Quantity gives quality—the best ideas really come from a high number of ideas—which really has been proven at Coca-Cola Enterprises Sweden during our improvement journey."

—Anna Greisz
Operations Director Supply Chain
Coca-Cola Enterprises Sweden

"*How to Succeed with Continuous Improvement* is a little gem with a large content! It defines why simplicity is of virtue for continuous improvement; even the book itself is a good practice of this with its easy-to-understand language and straightforward message. Being an engaging book that everybody can read and find useful regardless of experience, it is one of very few that actually delivers what it promotes. Unlike many other books on this subject, you only have to read it once because it sticks. Its reflecting short story format is appealing and easy to relate to, with a profound content that definitely grows on you and that you will continue to explore long after as if it were one of your own experiences."

—Johan Valett
Vice President Haldex Way
Haldex

"Reading *How to Succeed with Continuous Improvement* is getting access to a journey of insight. From realizing the importance of knowing where you are and getting effective tools to change to, finally, understanding how something as elusive as company culture can be approached on a deeper level."

—Henrik Fellesson
Group Controller
Scania

"Continuous improvement is about learning and improving as soon as you get the opportunity to do so—the one ability to focus on if you want to build a creative organizational culture. This book encapsulates the essence of how well-managed companies achieve astonishing results through people, and it is truly a must-read for managers and employees in both manufacturing and service organizations."

—Katalin Paldeak Pålsson
Vice President
Clarion Hotels

"This book is a must-have for both managers and employees in companies wanting to succeed with continuous improvements. Joakim tells his story in a way that makes it easy to understand and adapt the work procedures, even for beginners. *How to Succeed with Continuous Improvement* has been the key inspiration helping us achieve world-class results through continuous improvements at Solid Park."

—**Johan Åkerlund**
CEO
Solid Park

"Who does not want to become best in the world? Joakim Ahlström provides you with his insights on how continuous improvements can be the starting point for a cultural change that involves everyone in your organization. However, the book also shows how leaders need to stop providing solutions and answers to make the cultural change happen. The role of the leader is to build trust, tell engaging stories about the future, and ask the whys. Follow Joakim's advice and keep it simple if you want to succeed!"

—**Kirsti Gjellan**
Managing Director
Pfizer Health

"I was thrilled all the way while reading this book. It is a great work on continuous improvement that we will definitely use to train all our employees."

—**Karunagaran Krishnan**
Operations Director
Camfil Farr Malaysia

"*How to Succeed with Continuous Improvement* gives you a practical and straightforward approach to creating widespread commitment to continuous improvement. Within Assa Abloy we have used it to train and involve our employees in turning problems into improvements. I recommend *How to Succeed with Continuous Improvement* to anyone who needs a fast and inspiring introduction to continuous improvement."

—**Janne Lundberg**
Global Lean Innovation Manager
Assa Abloy

"*How to Succeed with Continuous Improvement* has given us a lot of inspiration in our improvement work! This easy-to-read book does not only show how improvement work can and should be common knowledge in an organization but also how it can become a fundamental part of the company culture. This book is a step-by-step guide to implement an improvement culture in an organization. The author, Joakim Ahlström, gives inspiring examples that make it almost impossible to stop reading the book before you are done."

—Anders Persson
Operations Development Manager
Ericsson

"This succinct book packs an enormous amount of wisdom and experience into an entertaining fast read. It gives a clear road map for any leader to implement a strong continuous improvement program in his or her unit. Highly recommended!"

—Alan G. Robinson
Professor of Management
University of Massachusetts
and author of *The Idea-Driven Organization*
and *Ideas Are Free*

"*How to Succeed with Continuous Improvement* is the perfect book to use in workgroups—especially those that need a kick start in their improvement work and problem solving. The author leads us through an easy-to-read story that provides very powerful tools and practical methods. I have had excellent experiences using this book and the effective concepts it provides."

—Mats Karlström
Lean Director
Saab Aerostructures

"A small book packed with big ideas. Highly practical, immensely relevant, and a great read!"

—Dr. Jonas Ridderstråle
Ranked as one of the top 50 business thinkers
globally and author of *Funky Business* and
Karaoke Capitalism

"Simplicity is the essence of this great book. Joakim Ahlström delivers a straightforward and simple approach to support your work with continuous improvement that creates significant results and dedicated coworkers."

—**Ronny Ålund**
Productivity Management
Volvo CE

"Joakim Ahlström has written a wonderful book about continuous improvement in organizations. It is well written, easy to read, and filled with excellent examples, great anecdotes, and quotes as well as several hands-on exercises. If you only plan to read one change management book this year, then this is the book you should read."

—**Dag Näslund**
Professor of Management
University of North Florida

"*How to Succeed with Continuous Improvement* demonstrates that continuous improvement can be very simple. With great success, we use tools and methods from the book to create energy and persistence in our effort to develop our business."

—**Joakim Danielsson**
Business Improvement Leader
Bombardier Transportation Sweden

"Just do it! Most of the time there are many excuses about why not to start improving right away. This book eliminates them all by showing how easy it is. Joakim captures it all when he asks where am I, where do I want to go, and how do I get there? So, if you are serious about improving, just start and learn while you improve. And if you get stuck—go back and read the book again."

—**Peter Palmér**
Senior Manager Process Support
Scania

"A great book that covers all critical elements of idea management in an entertaining story."

—**Dean M. Schroeder**
Professor of Management
Valparaiso University
and author of *The Idea-Driven Organization*
and *Ideas Are Free*

"The inspiration and easy-to-use tools Joakim and this book have given us have taken our work with continuous improvement to a higher level."

—Annika Mattsson
Finance Services Manager
IKEA

"This is an amusing and amazing guide in lean principles, with simple tools for simplifications. It's the perfect gift to your colleagues for your joint trip from good to great!"

—Susanne Schipper
Continuous Improvement Coach
AstraZeneca

HOW TO SUCCEED WITH CONTINUOUS IMPROVEMENT

HOW TO **SUCCEED**
WITH **CONTINUOUS**
IMPROVEMENT

A PRIMER FOR BECOMING
THE BEST IN THE WORLD

JOAKIM AHLSTRÖM

New York   Chicago   San Francisco   Athens   London   Madrid
Mexico City   Milan   New Delhi   Singapore   Sydney   Toronto

4 5 6 7 8 9 10 LCR 21 20 19 18 17

ISBN   978-0-07-183523-7
MHID   0-07-183523-7

e-ISBN 978-0-07-183524-4
e-MHID   0-07-183524-5

Library of Congress Cataloging-in-Publication Data

Ahlstrom, Joakim.
      How to succeed with continuous improvement : a primer for becoming the best in the world / Joakim Ahlstrom. — 1 Edition.
        pages cm
        ISBN 978-0-07-183523-7 (hardback : alk. paper) — ISBN 0-07-183523-7 1. Total quality management. 2. Continuous improvement process. 3. Success in business. I. Title.
      HD62.15.A386 2014
      658.4'09—dc23

                                                                                          2014029565

Illustrations: Michael Gustafsson, Nordinform

McGraw-Hill Education books are available at special quantity discounts to use as premiums and sales promotions or for use in corporate training programs. To contact a representative, please visit the Contact Us pages at www.mhprofessional.com.

To TEA

Contents

Foreword

By Karen Martin

Shingo Award–Winning Author of *The Outstanding Organization*

Over the years, hundreds of people have asked me which one book I'd recommend they read to understand the basics of continuous improvement. Each time, I struggled to answer this seemingly simple question. The book that people have been wanting and needing—an easy-to-read overview that's both comprehensive and industry-agnostic—simply didn't exist.

Most improvement books written to date have focused on a specific sector (e.g., manufacturing, healthcare, government) or job function (e.g., accounting, sales, IT), or they've been dense academic books best suited for improvement specialists, or they've been single-subject books that focus on specific improvement practices and tools (e.g., hoshin planning, value stream mapping, 5S, A3, pull systems). Leaders at all levels of an organization and people who are dedicated to improvement need a place to start that demonstrates the significant benefits of creating a true continuous improvement culture and provides a clear path forward.

Enter Joakim Ahlström. I met Joakim over a year ago when he was the host at an improvement conference I keynoted at in Stockholm, Sweden. I was immediately struck by Joakim's deep understanding about continuous improvement, and with lean management, specifically.

After the conference, Joakim shared with me a "little" 80-page book he had written and self-published that packed the biggest punch I'd ever seen in a book on improvement. *How to Succeed with*

Continuous Improvement reflected Joakim's view of what continuous improvement is really about, how organizations can succeed, and how they can avoid the pitfalls that often derail well-intended efforts. As I turned each page, I was convinced that *this* was the book that organizations have needed all along. Better late than never.

While *How to Succeed with Continuous Improvement* is written as a novel, there's nothing fictional about the content. Joakim's work with dozens of organizations—including Coca-Cola, Volvo, Ericsson, and IKEA—has given him the real-world experience that fills these pages. He's seen organizations soar, and he's seen organizations fail in their attempts to achieve excellence. Joakim clearly knows what works and what doesn't.

How to Succeed with Continuous Improvement will take you through the process from deciding to take the journey to creating a continuous improvement culture to reaping the results. It lays out a fail-proof framework for changing mindsets, the core of any continuous improvement journey. Of particular note is the chapter on how to shift mindsets and behaviors through the essential and often neglected practice of coaching. You may want to read the final chapter on cultural pitfalls first to help you think ahead about how you will apply the principles and practices that Joakim introduces throughout the book in your organization.

By the time you reach the end of this powerful primer, you will have learned how to use "six-legged spiders" and "fishy" diagrams to achieve measurable results and how to avoid "Watermelon KPIs" (key performance indicators) that mask the truth. *How to Succeed with Continuous Improvement* is now required reading for all of my new clients and recommended reading for the students, webinar attendees, workshop participants, social media contacts, and audience members I come into contact with.

Establishing a continuous improvement culture takes the right intention, proper know-how, and patient persistence. Armed with Joakim's inspiring and practical guide, you are in a powerful position to win.

Your Organizational Transformation Begins Here

The Problems and How Everything Started

Three years into my five-year graduate program in industrial and management engineering, I was expected to decide on an area of specialization. There were many different options to choose from, including marketing, logistics, and something called quality management. I found it difficult to make a decision because I thought all of them sounded interesting, but I knew that if I went for quality management, I would get to travel to Rome to finish my studies. You could say that this made my decision easier, and after a term of studies in Rome (which also helped to improve my knowledge of food, wine, coffee, and soccer), I headed back to Sweden.

I was not really sure what I wanted to do next, so I contacted my university and learned that a small IT company had called earlier that day, asking if there was anyone who could help with its improvement work. I visited the company, and to my great surprise I was immediately offered a one-year fixed-term contract to work on a project under the IT company's quality manager, Roger.

A Company with Problems

The IT company employed just under 100 people. Its business concept was to make sure that its customers did not have to spend any of their own time or resources on their IT.

The only things that its customers had to have were computers with Internet access and passwords. They should then be able to use everything they needed without any problems, including file servers, customer databases, e-mail programs, and so on.

The IT company and some of its customers

The IT company had been doing quite well. It had been growing steadily and employed some of the best IT staff in the region. One of its leading employees was Jonny, the head of the Operations and Customer Support groups. He was a company legend because he was able to understand computers and fix any problems more quickly than anyone else. The only negative thing about Jonny was that he sometimes made it clear that he thought he knew how to do things better than his colleagues.

Heroes Are a Sign of Weakness

Before Jonny went on vacation there was always a sense of panic in the air. Colleagues ran around, pulling Jonny here and there, wanting to check and make sure that everything was fine before he went away. It started to dawn on me that this was a sign that everything was not right at the IT company.

Jonny had become an organizational hero, and the fact that he had become so indispensable showed that the company's processes and work procedures had not been properly developed and were not stable enough.

In addition to Jonny, the management team at the IT company had six other members. They were the managing director, Eric, who had worked his way up the company ladder and knew virtually everyone who worked there personally; the sales manager, Stefan, a friendly solutions guy who was far more interested in starting projects than completing them; Nadia, a positive and very chatty person, who was responsible for sales support; the company's finance manager, Lena, a competent but cautious woman who could sometimes be heard saying, "Surely we can't do that, can we?"; Peter, the company's purchasing manager, who loved technology and the opportunities it brought; and finally, Roger, my manager and the company's quality manager, a practical humanist, who was a firm believer in people's ability.

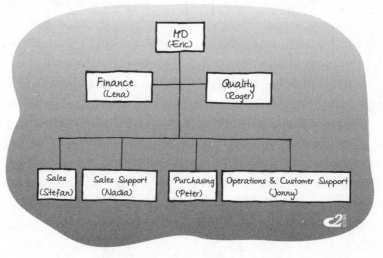

The IT company's organizational chart

One of the first things I was told when I got to the IT company was that it had recently seen a change of trend in its turnover. The previous quarter was the first quarter ever in the company's history when the number of new customers was lower than the number of customers that had decided to stop using the services of the IT company. This fact confirmed what the management team had suspected for some time: the company had serious problems.

Why Hadn't Anyone Done Anything About the Problem?

As a way of settling in, I suggested to my manager that we could start by having a look at the current improvement work of the IT company. We started walking around to the various departments, asking the employees about their improvement work.

"Improvements? We work with improvements all the time. In fact, it's basically the only thing we do all day," was the answer we received. We thought this sounded good to start with. But when we were given virtually the same answer at every department, we started to get suspicious and began looking for proof.

"Could you give us one or two examples of improvements that you have carried out recently?" we asked. This proved to be a provocative question, and suddenly our colleagues seemed less happy to have us as visitors. When we ran into Eric, the managing director, in the corridor, we asked him to describe an improvement that he had made recently.

"No problem!" he said. "Now, which one should I choose?" He stopped and thought for a little while and then gave the following answer. "I knew that we were going to have problems keeping our customers, even before we saw this in our statistics," he began. "I'd seen a negative trend in our availability logs for some time. So just under a year ago I decided to buy brand-new servers for our operations. They cost more than $400,000, and I think it was a really important improvement."

"We Carry Out Improvements All the Time"

If you ask the employees in an organization to name a few concrete examples of improvements they have made recently, it will show you whether improvements really are an integral part of their everyday work. If the people working there cannot provide you with any small, simple examples, it tells you that the organization does not have an improvement culture.

After talking with Eric, we checked with the people in operations to see how things were going with the new servers. We realized that most employees actually thought that the new servers had made things worse. They also claimed that downtime—the time customers were not able to access and use their systems—had in fact gone up, not down.

One Big Step Forward, Many Small Steps Back

Major changes, no matter if they occur as a result of changes in the surrounding world or due to internal decisions, often fail. A common reason is that there is no one who feels responsible for and is used to carrying out all the small changes and modifications that are needed to adapt to and secure the major change.

Management had started to take further action, which was proof that the situation had not really improved. Over the past six months it had started to display diagrams with monthly statistics of all registered downtime in visible places across the company. The idea was to show everyone how bad things were and to make it clear that something had to be done if the IT company was going to keep its customers.

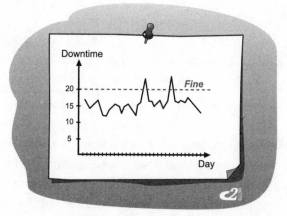

Diagram showing downtime and the fine limit

The diagram spoke for itself. Far too often customers were not able to access their systems. Having a diagram that showed the limit for when a fine was imposed was a way of visualizing what the IT company had agreed on with its customers. Most customer agreements stated that the IT company would not be paid for its services if the total downtime on one day was more than the agreed limit of 20 minutes. When Roger and I saw the diagram, we felt quite uneasy. We started to discuss what the diagram meant for the IT company's employees and our customers. We decided to rephrase the questions we had been asking our colleagues. Instead of talking about improvements, we tried to find out how the employees felt and discover what signals our colleagues were getting from our customers. We summarized our analysis in bullet form, and the results clearly showed we had a challenge in front of us.

Internal (our employees)

Stress
Dejection/Powerlessness
Fear of losing job
Thoughts of moving
/Looking for new job
Denial/Blaming others
Aggression/Conflicts

External (our customers)

Irritation
Work disrupted
Change of supplier
Thinking of changing supplier
Stress/Uncertainty
Losing business/money

How the employees and customers were affected

Our colleagues had painted quite a negative picture of the situation as a whole. Not only were we not performing well enough as a company, the employees were not happy at work either, and this was having an effect on what our customers thought of us. We kept on finding new evidence showing that things were not as good as they should be. Some employees had been off sick because they were burned out, and competent employees had left the company and moved over to competitors. When we sat down to drink coffee with our colleagues during breaks, the conversations constantly turned into moaning about other departments and complaining about their lack of competence. People were blaming each other at all levels of the company. The operations department was performing badly because the purchasing department was buying such bad software and hardware; the salespeople could not make sales because of the quality of the operations, and so on.

There was one question that started to bug me. We had competent and experienced people working at the IT company and all of them wanted to do a good job, yet problems had still been allowed to take on huge proportions. If everything was as bad as people were saying, why had no one done anything about it?

Improvement Work Is like Orienteering

It was clear that most people in the company were aware that we were having problems. Management had also realized that the methods they had used to deal with these problems were not effective in the long run. Roger, the quality manager, had therefore been given the job of doing something about the situation, and I was supposed to help him. Roger was a good-hearted and reserved thinker whose major passion in life was orienteering. I once heard him describe the sport as a compelling mix of brainpower, fitness, decision making, and a chance to appreciate nature.

I, as all Swedes, had practiced some orienteering in school, but to me Roger's portrayal was a bit over the top. My recollection of orienteering was as a navigation race in unfamiliar terrain where you used a map and a compass to find your way between checkpoints. I often wished Roger would speak less about orienteering when we were trying to get to grips with how to approach our challenging situation. I thought our assignment—to start an improvement process that would make the IT company competitive again—was difficult enough, but to make matters worse Roger insisted that we have some kind of orienteering theme for the improvement program we were going to set up. "If only we could get everyone to think like orienteers," I heard him muttering to himself from time to time. For me, Roger's talk of orienteering sounded like incoherent rambling. I did not understand what he meant, and my irritation grew the more orienteering references he made.

We decided to go to a conference to get some inspiration and advice on what we should do next. There were many different conferences to choose from, but Roger decided on a two-day conference that included improvement experts and practical case studies from companies that had come a long way with their improvement work. At the beginning of the conference, I was not inspired at all. The people who took to the stage seemed to live in a completely different reality compared to the work environment that I knew. I could not see how we at the IT company could possibly start working like them or achieve the level they had reached. The only thing that did encourage me was that some speakers indicated that their situation had been like ours before they started making improvements. However, they had started to make these changes so long ago that no one was really clear about what to do to start the process.

On the second day there was a speaker named Jeffrey Liker. He had been studying Toyota for a long time, and everyone there seemed to think that Toyota was the best company in the world when it came to continuous improvement.

I thought that if anyone could help us get started, it was him. So when it was time for questions, I decided to ask for advice.

"We don't know how to get started," I began. "We have major problems, but we don't know how to tackle them. We can't even agree on what we mean by an improvement," I added in frustration. I had not intended to say this. It had just come out, and I felt I had not properly framed the question about how to get started.

Instead Jeffrey started to speak. He said that we needed patience, and he recommended taking it in small steps. He also told us that Toyota defined an improvement as a problem solved.

This all sounded good and simple, I thought. But Jeffrey did not stop there. He added that a problem at Toyota was defined as the gap between where you were and where you wanted to be.

It took a while before it all sank in, but when I looked at Roger, I could see that he had heard something he liked. His face had lit up, and suddenly I realized what Roger had been talking about. You cannot make an improvement if you do not know where you are at the moment and have a clear target. Just like when you are out in the forest orienteering, you always need to know where you are in relation to your target.

When the conference was over, Roger and I were finally able to agree that our job was to get everyone at the IT company to ask these three orienteering questions as often as possible:

1. Where am I?
2. Where am I going?
3. How am I going to get there?

Three orienteering questions

Now that Roger and I were really inspired, I wanted to go and tell our colleagues immediately that everything was going to be all right, as long as all of them started to think like orienteers. I could see that Roger hesitated.

"First we need to give everyone time to think about what this means for them," he said tentatively. "Before we do anything else we have to hold training sessions to discuss the purpose of improvement work. Then we will give everyone the chance to try it out in practice," he added more confidently. I realized that he was right and that we had to make sure that we avoided the trap of "more haste, less speed."

Analysis of the Problem

Why had no one done anything about the problem? This is a central question when working with improvements. The answer will lead you to what gets people engaged and motivated to address important issues.

Why Had No One Done Anything About the Problem?

Feedback on what they have done plays a decisive role in how people act in the future. Although the employees at the IT company did receive feedback, it was not done in a constructive way. They were presented with a graph showing the joint result of everyone at the company, and the graph always showed the result of the previous month. Since the results were compiled for the company as a whole and so much time had passed, it was virtually impossible for the company's employees to see how they as individuals had affected the results.

No one ever went up to the diagram at the beginning of September and said, "That's true—the third of August was a good day. I remember exactly what I was doing then and can see how this might have affected the results." Or "All right, now I see. Things didn't turn out so well on the twelfth. So now, four weeks down the line, maybe we should sit down and think about what might have caused this." Instead of encouraging people to take positive action, the effect of this feedback was to make them feel even more negative and powerless.

"Too Much Talk, Not Enough Do"

General Electric legend Jack Welch has an often-quoted expression: "Too much talk, not enough do." In other words, the main reason companies do not succeed is that they spend too much time talking instead of doing. I agree with him in many respects. Indeed, it is a mistake that I have made myself. I have spent time talking about different improvement approaches, losing time and energy arguing which one is the best one to use. This creates uncertainty in organizations and undermines confidence in future initiatives.

Taking the first steps into the unknown may seem frightening, particularly if it means that you might come up against opposition or make mistakes. In comparison talking is a safe activity, but if you want to make a real difference you need to stop talking and start making improvements. Improvement work is about learning from your mistakes and developing. So the best improvement method is the one that you and your colleagues decide on, keep to, and continuously improve. As long as your approach is easy to grasp and use, and it helps you to move toward your targets, it makes no difference what you call it. At the IT company we called it orienteering.

The Activities That Started the Improvement Work

We had a simple objective with our training—we wanted to explain two main concepts and, of course, get everyone thinking like orienteers. We also wanted the people taking part in the training to talk more than we, the people giving the training, did. We carried out the training department by department and made sure that each session did not last more than 45 minutes. We held the first session with the sales support department.

"Why should we work with improvements?" Roger began. He asked the meeting attendees to discuss this question in pairs. There were many different answers, everything from making sure they kept their jobs to making their everyday work easier. What the answers were was less important than making sure all participants had at least one answer of their own that they found meaningful.

"Unnecessary Hassle"

Roger then told the group that he had given me a task to carry out. Afterward they would be asked to define what my task had been. They should also measure the time it took me to carry it out.

I sat on a chair. The group chose a person to time me, and when this person told me to start, I got up and began walking across the room. Everyone could see that I was heading toward a flipchart, but to get there I first had to move a table that was in my way. When I had done this, I reached for a pen that should have been on the stand under the pad. But it was not there, so I had to go over to a desk that was a little farther away and look for a pen that was in one of the drawers. I then went back to the flipchart and wrote the word *Value* in green pen on the pad, threw the pen to one side, went back to the chair, and sat down.

A task made difficult by unnecessary hassle

"How long did it take?" asked Roger.

"Thirty seconds," answered the person who was timing me.

"What did you think the task was?" continued Roger. A blank expression appeared on the faces of our colleagues. The silence lasted for a little while. Then someone tried, a little tentatively:

"Writing the word *Value* on the pad?"

"Completely right," answered Roger.

"How long did the actual writing take?"

"Maybe three seconds," answered the same person.

"All right," said Roger, "around 10 percent of the time. If you were all going to help Joakim to do his job more quickly, what would you suggest?" The participants now started to understand what the exercise was about.

"Move the chair closer to the flipchart!" suggested one person.

"Make sure the pen is always in the right place," said another.

"Make sure the table is not in the way at the start," added a third.

"Does he really need to be sitting down?" asked someone who had been quiet up until this point.

"You are tough, but that's true, he doesn't have to be," agreed Roger.

"So now we've gotten rid of the unnecessary walking, cleared all the clutter, and made sure that Joakim does not have to go looking for his tools. Is there anything else you can think of?" he then asked.

"Hold the pen and take the top off in advance," someone suggested, before quickly changing her mind. "Actually, keep the top on to make sure the pen doesn't dry out."

"All right," said Roger. "Let's try again." I wrote again and they timed me. This time it took only five seconds.

Ninety-Five Percent of What You Do Is Pure Waste

In his book *Lean Production Simplified*, Pascal Dennis writes that 95 percent of the time in a normal company is spent on non-value-adding activities. After working systematically for decades to remove waste (or unnecessary hassle) from their processes, some successful companies can pride themselves on having more than 30 percent value-adding time in their processes. How big is the potential in your company?

"Thank you for helping me make my job easier," I carried on, still in character.

"But there is something I'm wondering about. When Roger asked you for advice about doing my task more quickly, none of you told me to write faster—why not?" They looked at me quizzically.

"It wouldn't have made that much difference," someone said.

"All right," I said. "So you're saying that the potential for me to speed up my work was not in the actual writing itself?"

"Exactly," came the reply.

"You might also have written incorrectly or illegibly if you'd written too quickly," said someone else.

"All right, and what would happen then?" Roger interjected.

"I'm sure you would have made him write it again," joked someone else.

"You can bet on that," said Roger. "But how would this have affected the total amount of time needed to carry out the task?"

Roger's question was rhetorical, and no one answered. Instead it triggered a lively discussion on the similarities between the situation I had just acted out and the situation at work that our colleagues experienced on a daily basis. Roger summarized the discussion by showing a diagram he had prepared on a flipchart. The diagram showed the common mistake of focusing improvement work on shortening the time spent on creating the value, that is, the time spent on activities that have a direct impact on customer satisfaction or an effect that the customer is willing to pay for.

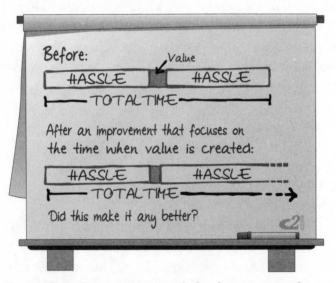

The problem of improvement work that focuses on employees working harder and machines going faster

After Roger had finished, I asked everyone to work in pairs again. This time they had to come up with concrete activities that they did to create value and to <u>provide examples</u> of unnecessary <u>hassle in their daily work</u>, the things preventing them from creating value.

When the pairs reported their discussions, I wrote what they said on the flipchart. I had one column for unnecessary hassle and one column for value. Everyone in the room agreed that it was easy to choose between speeding up the activities in the value column and removing what was listed in the unnecessary hassle column.

To end the discussion on unnecessary hassle, we gave everyone three votes. We told them to look through the list of unnecessary hassle and place their votes on the hassle they, the people in the sales support department, should address first. We were careful to word it in a way that did not allow for votes on unnecessary hassle that they thought someone else caused and that someone else should work to remove.

Unnecessary hassle	Value
Waiting ///	Providing installation data
Uneven workload	Creating a prospect list
Machine/Computer stoppage	
Reworking/Repairing//	
Overburden	
Wrong information/Asking	
Unclear plan	
Lack of material or data ////	
Searching/Disorder //////	
Unnecessary meetings/activities	

Unnecessary hassle and value-creating activities. The hassle of searching/disorder received the most votes to be addressed first.

Internal Customers

Unnecessary hassle was a simple concept that our colleagues in all the departments easily understood and were prepared to work hard to remove. To us the expression "unnecessary hassle" clarified both that we should focus on our most obvious problems first and that creating value would sometimes not be completely effort-less. Once we had identified the different kinds of hassle and voted on which one the department was going to tackle first, we continued the training with our simple role playing.

"Now some of you are probably starting to suspect that the task Roger has given me is made up," I started jokingly, "but I've just realized that I did something wrong the last time I wrote on the flipchart. What could I have done wrong?" I asked.

"What do you mean wrong? How are we going to know that?" one of the men in the room exclaimed, making it clear that he thought my guessing games had started to get more than a little silly.

"I'm talking in general; what kinds of errors could I have made in this situation?" I tried to clarify.

"Wrong color," someone shouted out, coming to my rescue. "Maybe it should have been blue instead of green."

"That's right," I said. "It should probably have been blue. Anything else?"

"Capital letters," added the man who had just been critical, much to my delight.

"Exactly," I said. "It should have been written in blue capital letters. Furthermore, I am quite tall, around six feet three inches. Could that have affected the results?"

"Sure, maybe the word should have been written in blue, with capital letters, and 15 inches lower on the flipchart," someone suggested, helping me to sum everything up.

"All right, you mean down here," I said, and wrote just as I had been instructed. "But who decides what is right?" I asked.

"That would be him, your boss," someone said and pointed at Roger.

"Really," said Roger. "Does everyone agree?"

"No, it's the customer, of course!" disagreed one of the colleagues.

"Thank you," said Roger, who seemed happy that all his "quality management talk" about customer focus had not been completely in vain.

Writing farther down the pad as requested by the customer

"But this doesn't feel very good," I said. "When I wrote down at the bottom of the flipchart, I was forced to bend over like a penknife, and if I had to keep on doing this, it would give me back pain. What can we do about this?" The suggestions came immediately.

"Get yourself an adjustable flipchart. Or sit down again. Then you could comfortably do what is needed to make the customer happy," someone proposed.

"Or we could saw your legs off. Or just employ someone who is more suitable," joked someone else.

"Thanks, but I prefer the first alternative," I said.

"Isn't improvement work easy?" I asked rhetorically. "This is exactly what improvement work is all about. First we ask what our customers want, and then we try to deliver that with as little hassle as possible for ourselves!"

Everyone agreed. No one thought it was complicated, and everyone thought it was important.

The principle for creating perfect flows

While I was summing up on the flipchart, a new discussion started about who the customer was and the best way to find out what your customers want. During our first training session with the sales support department, we realized that there were many different customer and supplier relationships within the IT company.

This realization made us start using the term *internal customers*, and we took it with us to the training sessions with the rest of our departments. Everyone also agreed that finding out what the customer wanted did not have to be difficult. "All you have to do is ask," as one of our colleagues put it.

Customer and supplier relationships in the flow at the IT company
Sales – Sales Support – Purchasing – Operations – Customer Support

You Could Stop Reading Here

Unnecessary hassle and internal customers. At the end of the day this is what it is all about. You don't actually need to know anything else. If you are able to get all your colleagues to identify and deliver what their (internal) customers want, while they are continually minimizing the amount of unnecessary hassle for themselves, you are on your way to creating a perfect flow. The way you do this—the actual method—is less important.

"Board Meetings"

At the IT company we realized that a "board meeting" was a simple and useful concept. To us it simply meant that every department was going to get a board, preferably a whiteboard, and hold meetings by it. We suggested that every department have a "board meeting" at least once a week that would last between 15 and 30 minutes. Our idea was for the "board meetings" to be based on the three questions of an orienteer and focus on removing the unnecessary hassle that prevented employees from working to make their internal (or external) customers happy. "Improvement meeting" might have described the purpose more clearly, but to us the fact that all of us should take part in regular board meetings symbolized an important link between all levels of the organization.

At the training sessions all of the departments had already voted on the kind of unnecessary hassle they wanted to tackle first. This meant that the problem area had already been defined. We now wanted all the members of each department to immediately work together to ask the three orienteering questions. But things rarely turn out the way you want them to.

Current State: Where Are We?

Roger and I had decided to be present at the first two "board meetings" of every department. We would hold the first meeting, and we would be there at the second meeting to offer any support that the department members needed. Sales support was the first department to hold a "board meeting."

The meeting was based on the type of hassle that had received the most votes from the people in sales support during their training session. We had saved their list of unnecessary hassle, and it showed that they had decided to reduce the amount of searching needed by making sure everything was neat, tidy, and well organized.

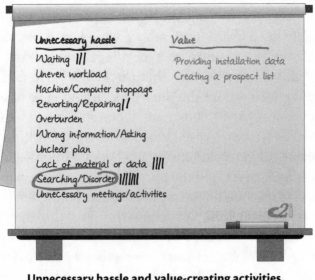

Unnecessary hassle and value-creating activities.
The hassle of searching/disorder had received
the most votes to be addressed first.

Roger started by asking if everyone remembered the first orienteering question. They all did—"Where are we?"

"But what does this question mean for us?" I asked the participants. No one answered, so Roger jumped in.

"How do we answer the question of where we are, when it comes to having a neat, tidy, and well-organized workplace? Can we identify where we are in terms of workplace organization today so that we can use this as our starting point?"

"We could measure how long it takes us to find things that are not in their right place," suggested one of the newer colleagues.

"Good suggestion," I said. "Any other ideas?"

"We could put everything where we want it to be and take photos. Then we can perform audits and calculate the number of deviations," said Nadia, head of sales support.

"Very good. That sounds like a structured approach," said Roger.

"Why spend so much time on measuring? Surely it'd be better to spend our energy on making improvements," objected Nils, one of the more experienced employees, before Roger had time to say anything else.

"I think you're right," answered Roger. "But maybe we could find a simple way of measuring that would give us a quick answer to the question," continued Roger, who was very eager to get all three orienteering questions answered during the meeting. But Nils did not hesitate to voice his next objection.

"Is it really something that can be measured? The issue of 'neat and tidy' is of course subjective. What's neat and tidy to me might not be neat and tidy to you." Roger now started to look a little under pressure, but Nadia came to his rescue.

"Yes, but we measure subjective issues, for example, in the employee surveys that we answer from time to time. Couldn't we use the same method here?" she wondered.

"So in this case we could all just put a score between one and five to show what we think about how neat and tidy things are in the department and then calculate the average. This would allow us to identify where we are without wasting a lot of time," said Nils triumphantly.

"Perfect!" I said. "That's what we'll do."

I gave everyone a Post-it note. They had to write a number between one and five on it—with one being the lowest score and five being the highest. We gave them 30 seconds to think and write, and during this time I drew a 1-to-5 scale on their improvement board. After less than two minutes all the Post-its had been put up on the board and the average had been calculated.

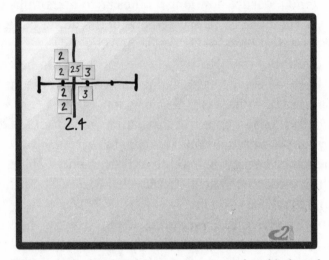

Survey result showing the current state on the whiteboard

Target: Where Are We Going?

What the second question—"Where are we going?"—meant in this situation was quite easy to see. It was natural for everyone to set a target to aim for. However, it was not easy to agree on what the target should be. For some people it was logical for the target to be the highest score possible—5.0—while others objected, saying that this was unreasonable, as everyone saw "neat and tidy" in a slightly different way. After a short discussion, the group agreed to set the target at 4.5.

Once the target had been visualized on the board, Roger asked if they could all see the problem they were facing. Most of them remembered the definition that a problem is the gap between the current state and the target. We were ready for the next step—to analyze the problem and decide how to get from our current state to our target.

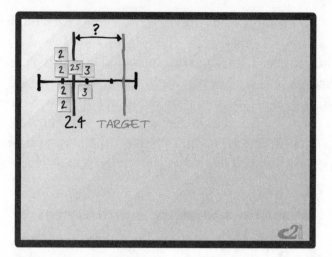

The problem is the gap between the current state and the target

Fishbone Diagrams: How Are We Going to Get There?

When I was at the university, I was taught about many different problem-solving tools. The one I remembered the most was the "fishbone" diagram. I did not remember exactly how to use it, but I remembered from the name how good fishbone diagrams were for dissecting problems. We wanted to decide on concrete action to move from our present situation to our target. We all agreed that the first thing we should do was to imagine what the situation would be like when we reached our target. We therefore started our fishbone exercise by asking the question, "Why aren't we scoring an average of 4.5 for 'neat and tidy'?" Once we had asked this question it became easy for everyone to identify the reasons they had not given higher marks for the current state.

Everyone wrote down their answers to the question on separate Post-it notes. They then read them out loud to each other. If answers were similar, they were grouped together on the same branch of the fishbone diagram. When all Post-it notes were put on the fishbone diagram, every branch was given a simple heading.

Then everyone placed a total of three votes each on the different branches of the fishbone—these branches were now potential improvement areas. Each participant voted by putting pen strokes on the branch or branches that they thought they as a group should tackle first. If they wanted, they could put all three votes on the same branch, but they could also choose to put their votes on different branches. The group then counted up the votes to see which area they should work on first.

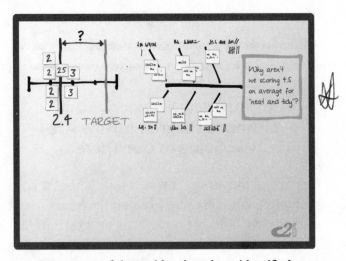

Root causes of the problem have been identified

Everyone in the group then came up with suggestions on how to improve this particular area. We realized that often we only had to read the Post-it notes on the branch to discover small and simple improvements. For example the note "Lots of clutter in the archive room" was transformed into the improvement activity "Clear out everything that we do not need in the archive room." We wrote each improvement activity on the group's to-do list. The to-do list showed what was going to be done, who was going to do it, and when it was going to be completed.

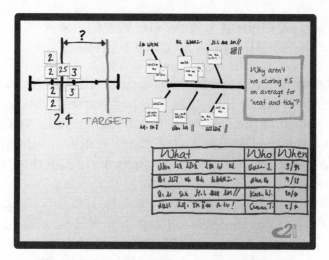

The to-do list is now in place on the whiteboard

To help the group produce fishbone diagrams on their own in the future I gave them a quick reference guide. With it they could produce a fishbone diagram in just 15 minutes.

Formulate the question: Focus the problem using a "Why" question — 1 minute

Individual work: Answer the question on Post-it notes (one reply per note) — 3 minutes

Spread out the notes: Group the notes and give the branches headings — 5 minutes

Have consensus through voting: Prioritize the root cause groups (branches) — 1 minute

Your to-do list: List solutions and the person responsible, including completion date — 5 minutes

Simple instructions for producing a fishbone diagram

Celebrate: How Do We Make It All the Way to the Target?

Our colleagues had been hesitant and skeptical at the beginning of the session, but by this stage they had started to become more positive. Some of them were getting quite excited, even making jokes about my excessive use of Post-it notes. I think this was because they could see how easy the working method was and that they would finally get the opportunity to improve processes that had been ignored for a long time. I thought this was a perfect moment to end our first session. But it turned out that not everyone was as satisfied as I was. Nils, the most skeptical participant, started speaking again:

"It sounds just great that you want us to work hard on this and ask ourselves these three questions over and over. But haven't we forgotten the most important question?"

"Really, Nils? What question is that?" I asked.

"How do we make sure we all have the energy to make it all the way to the target?" said Nils with a grin on his face.

Fortunately you sometimes get help to make sure your original idea turns out even better than you planned. This was one of those occasions. One of the biggest skeptics helped us develop our approach. He added a very important dimension—to set subtargets and celebrate along the way to the final target. We spent five minutes discussing suitable subtargets and how the department members as a group were going to celebrate when they reached them. Since Nadia, who was in charge of the department's budget, took part in the meeting, she could immediately say yes to the proposed ways of celebrating.

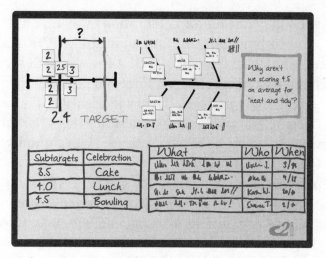

Subtargets and ways of celebrating complete the board

However, some managers who were in charge of budgets were skeptical about the celebration aspect. There were even a few who calculated how much it was going to cost the company if everyone achieved their targets! We thought this was a strange way to look at things—it made it sound negative to achieve our targets. But to silence the skeptics, we introduced two criteria for celebrations. The first was that the department or group had to celebrate together. For example, they could not give movie tickets to the group members to use by themselves whenever they wanted—they all had to go to the movies together. The whole idea was to enforce team spirit and solidarity.

Positive results and completed improvements are celebrated in the team

The second criterion for celebrations was that at least two "PARs" had to be produced and submitted. PAR stands for "Problem, Activity, and Results," and it is a way of describing an improvement on a sheet of paper. First you describe the problem and the extent of the problem. Then you describe what was done to solve the problem, and finally you describe the achieved results. We encouraged everyone to use pictures, simple graphs, and figures instead of writing long texts.

The problem section in one of the simpler PARs showed a picture of an untidy office. The activity part showed a person sorting out rubbish and organizing material and equipment, while the results part showed a picture of a clean and well-organized office, with everything in its right place. A more controversial, but also appreciated, PAR only contained a few words and figures: "50%" was in the problem box, "purpose, information, training" was in the activity box, and "90%" was in the results box. Everyone at the IT company knew what this meant, but it was cryptic to say the least for an outsider. Since we put up every PAR on a big bulletin board inside the main entrance to the IT company, and this PAR was quite eye-catching, we often had to explain to our visitors what it meant.

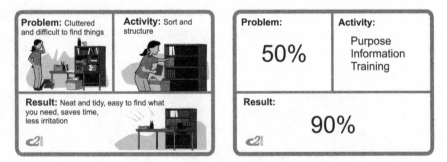

Two examples of PAR—Problem, Activity, and Result

Here is the background. There had been a lot of errors and rework in connection with new installations because the salespeople were not using the order template. They were supposed to use this template to inform the technicians about the details regarding the services a new customer wanted. The technicians were there-fore the salespeople's internal customers. Although the company had talked about both internal and external customers and sup-pliers, it was clear that the salespeople had not fully understood the needs of their internal customers. So the technicians decided to do something about it. They started to measure how often the salespeople used the order templates. One day when the sales-people were going to have a meeting they found a note on their improvement board with the heading "customer satisfaction" and the figure "50%."

If you think that this was well received, then think again. When they had managed to figure out where the note came from, a couple of salespeople went with the note to the technicians and demanded to know what was going on. They were met by a smiling colleague who was prepared for their arrival.

"It's great that you've seen our survey," she started. "As you know, there have been quite a few errors in our new installations recently. We think that one reason is that you're not using the order template we designed together. That's why we've started measur-ing how often you use it." In spite of the disarming response, the salespeople felt attacked.

"What template are you talking about?" they asked.

"Thank you for asking. Here is the template," said the techni-cian, holding up a piece of paper. "I've already printed out a pile of them for you to put in your break room. We've also put it on the intranet, so you can access it when you're out on the road." The salespeople now started to calm down slightly.

"All right, but have you thought about how you would like us to fill in all these boxes?" they sighed.

"We'll do it like this," said the technician. "Let's go back to your colleagues and go through the template. I will answer any ques-tions you might have, and I promise to write down the answers to your questions so you can keep them as a quick guide."

At the salespeople's request the technician told them the pur-pose of the template and the problems caused by not using it, where the template could be found, and how to fill it in. The percentage of completed templates gradually increased. In just a few months, new surveys showed that the salespeople were using the template 90 percent of the time, and errors in new installations fell by almost the same amount.

Steal as Much as You Can

Have you ever felt like you are the only one suffering from a certain problem, but then found out that there are lots of people with exactly the same problem as you? At the IT company, everyone thought that his or her department was struggling with unique problems, but when the good examples of completed improvements were visualized, we could see that almost everyone had similar problems. Therefore we were able to copy each other's solutions. The value of our improvements was multiplied by the fact that they were carried out in several sections of the company.

Analysis of the Activities

Command-and-control management makes people feel deprived of their freedom and can result in employees asserting their autonomy by resisting every single change, even when the change might be to their benefit.

Everyone Wants to Take Part in Creating the World He or She Will Live In

The easiest way of avoiding resistance to change is to ask people what they think rather than tell them what to do. At the IT company everyone was given the chance to raise problems they were experiencing and to vote on which problem they would work to solve first. Did this affect their willingness to take part in the improvement work? Of course! But what about the people who thought that another problem was more important (and not the one that got the most votes)? They still chose to take part for two reasons. First, they had been a part of the whole process and had been given a chance to affect the outcome—it is often more important to have your voice heard than to get your own way. And second, their problems were still on the list and they would also be addressed in time.

Not More Meetings but More Effective Meetings

Normally you do not need more meetings—most organizations already have enough. The challenge is to make the meetings you already have more effective. Make sure your meetings focus on the right things—where you stand in relation to your targets and what has to be done to bridge the gap between your current state and your targets. To be more precise you should have "board meetings" focusing on improvements that each section of your organization needs to carry out to ensure that your company as a whole achieves its objectives.

Some people say that they do not have enough time to work with improvements. When we came across this attitude at the IT company we started the improvement work by concentrating on the unnecessary hassle that our colleagues said took the most time away from them. From a company perspective it is also important to remember what happens when you do not take the time to make improvements: you do not get better. And what happens to those who do not get better? In an ever-changing world and with tougher competition, they stop being good. Or as quality guru Edward Deming has been known to say: "No one has to change, survival is optional."

Are You Ready to Confront the Harsh Reality?

At the IT company we started all "board meetings" by looking at the current state. The purpose of a current state analysis is to create a starting point for improvements. It does not have to be complicated, but if the current state analysis does not reflect reality, the subsequent measures will at worst be useless. If the current state analysis is insightful and based on facts, it is easier to identify the most effective improvements.

One of the world's most popular management books is called *Good to Great: Why Some Companies Make the Leap . . . and Others Don't*. In this book, the author, Jim Collins, says that the best companies in the world are the ones that look truth right in the eye and take the necessary action. Successful businesses' decisions are not based on preconceptions or vague suppositions. The successful businesses are the ones that confront the harsh reality and base their decisions on facts.

This is a question of attitude. Try looking closely at how you and your colleagues approach reality. Do you often spend time fretting that things did not turn out the way you wanted them to, talk about how great it would be if your reality was slightly different, or discuss why there probably is something wrong with the most recent customer survey? Do you spend more time on this than on deciding on and carrying out the actions required by the situation?

What Can We Influence?

It did not take long before fishbone diagrams became a natural part of the improvement work at the IT company. We started to use them wherever we saw the opportunity: when something went wrong ("Why did X go wrong?"), if we did not reach a target ("Why didn't we reach target Y?"), or when we received the results from a customer or employee survey ("Why didn't we get higher marks for question Z?"). We learnt that it was essential for us to focus on the root causes (the branches in the fishbone) that we could influence. When looking at ways to move forward, we never considered voting on or spending energy on any root causes that we thought should be solved by someone else.

Producing fishbone diagrams was mostly a way for us to create consensus. Basing action on facts and finding the root causes of the problem was an important part of it, but perhaps even more important was the fact that everyone could make his or her voice heard, in a democratic process where we moved quickly from words to actions. We worked to find the right balance between precision and tempo and soon realized that the one who is quick to act is also quick to correct, and the one who only analyzes never moves forward.

Getting the Right Things Done

After I had left the IT company I found the following diagram in the book *Getting the Right Things Done* by Pascal Dennis. Pascal has worked in and supported many world-class organizations in their improvement work, and according to him the diagram illustrates the core of all improvement work. This diagram confirmed that we had used the right approach at the IT company.

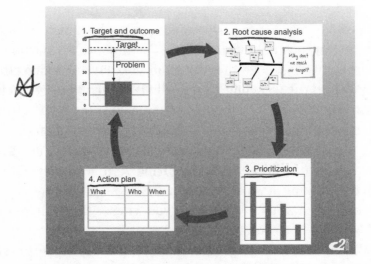

The "improvement loop" from the book *Getting the Right Things Done*
by Pascal Dennis

Success Breeds Success Factors

Do you think it is more fun when things are going well than when they are going badly? That is what we thought at the IT company. When we started to visualize the good examples of improvements that we had carried out, it spread a positive feeling that we were doing something good, that we were successful.

Tests have been carried out in which two groups were asked to analyze information and predict the price development of a number of stocks. No matter how well they performed, one group was told that their forecast was good and was close to the actual outcome, while the other group was told that their forecast was bad. When the two groups, which had actually performed equally well, were asked to describe their work, the "successful" group said that they had worked in a committed and structured way, had open communication, and supported each other. The members of the second group said that they had worked in an unstructured way, had difficulty getting started, people had talked over each other, and they had pulled in different directions. However, the external observers had not seen any differences in the way the groups had worked.

There is always more than one way to look at a situation, and from this experiment we learn that we, by always having a positive and productive perspective, will not only help others do the same, but they will also adjust their self-image and behavior to fit our expectations.

All You Have to Do Is Ask

Think about the opportunities that arise when everyone shares his or her opinions and ideas. At the IT company we learned to appreciate when our colleagues were open with their opinions and voiced their skepticism. It made us strengthen our arguments and allowed us to deal with the concerns people had before they grew out of proportion. Often all you have to do is ask for people's thoughts or ideas. Sometimes you have to do more. One way of asking indirectly is to start measuring. Measuring sets the focus on a specific issue, and it can have unforeseen consequences. When something is measured and visualized, it is perceived as important, and when we perceive something as important, it affects how we talk and act.

Results and Success Factors

From the very first "board meeting" with sales support, every department asked four questions at their meetings. First they asked where they were and measured their current state. They then asked where they were going and set a target. After this they asked how they were going to get there and broke down the problem and identified concrete improvement activities. And finally they asked how they were going to stay motivated and decided how they were going to celebrate their successes along the way.

Everyone Started to Do Something About the Problems

As time went by and people got used to these meetings, many groups started to have shorter meetings more frequently. As targets did not change very often and measurements could be done before the meeting, many meetings were limited to short root cause analysis and decisions on what measures to take. This simple working method allowed us to speed up the pace of our improvement work quite quickly.

The company's major problem, and the main reason I had been employed, was the downtime in its customers' systems. In spite of major investments, the IT company had not been able to get to the bottom of this problem. All groups within the operations department decided to focus their improvement work on the unnecessary hassle of downtime or "machine stoppages" as they called it. Almost everyone in all groups agreed that the stoppages in the systems were what annoyed them the most in their daily work.

Unnecessary hassle	Value
Lack of material or data	Delivering user accounts
Reworking/Repairing ‖	Updating software
Machine/Computer stoppage ‖‖‖‖	
Lack of space	
Overloading	
Wrong information	
Unclear instructions/expectations	
Waiting ‖	
Searching/Disorder ‖	
Unnecessary meetings/activities ‖	

The hassle of machine stoppages received the most votes for improvement

However, we almost didn't get past the first question in the first group. How were we going to measure this? The group's first idea was to time how long the system was down using a stopwatch. But some people thought this was too complicated. There were quite heated discussions about what method to use. Just when things felt the most hopeless, someone came up with the suggestion of asking the customers—they would be the final judges anyway! I felt quite embarrassed that I had not thought of this idea myself, but all I could do was encourage the initiative. Everyone in the group phoned a customer and asked for his or her view on downtime problems. The answers they received surprised most people at the IT company.

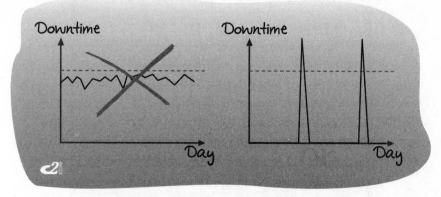

Two possible cases, highlighting the customers' wants

It was not the major system breakdowns that were the problem—our customers were more irritated by the short, frequent stoppages. At the IT company we had thought that everything was all right provided any small stoppages were fixed before passing the limit when fines were given. We had actually taken pride in our ability to stay below the limit most of the time. We realized that this misinterpretation had given us the wrong focus. At the end of the day a stoppage was a stoppage, and we had to remove all of them. When we knew that the frequency of the stoppages was the most important factor, not the length of the stoppage, the group decided to measure them by putting a pen stroke on the board every time there was a stoppage.

The group measured stoppages for a week and then decided that their target should be a maximum of two stops a week. I thought this was too ambitious and did not believe that they were going to achieve it—they had previously had around 10 stops per shift—but I did not want to dampen their enthusiasm. The operations group produced a fishbone diagram by asking, "Why don't we have a maximum of two stops per week?" Then they went through all improvement areas in the fishbone diagram systematically and in order of priority.

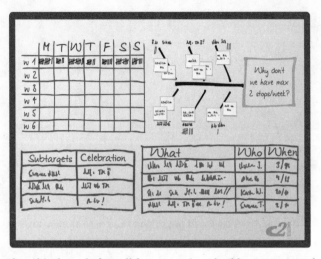

The whiteboard after all four questions had been answered

The group carried out almost all the activities on their to-do list. After just over six months and several fishbone diagrams later, they reached their final target. All of our operations groups used the same approach, and all achieved performance levels most of us had believed were impossible. An important reason for the fast progress was the sharing of lessons and improvements between the groups.

One year after the first "board meeting," the whole operations department decided to celebrate its successes together. The department members went on a study visit to one of Europe's most respected companies in the IT sector. The fact that the company had a facility in Spain, with its fine climate and good food and drink, might have influenced the choice of destination a little.

We were happy and proud of the changes we made at the IT company. Many of us were surprised by our ability to achieve results together. Before I finished at the IT company, I often talked with Roger and my other colleagues about why we had been able to achieve so much so quickly. What had contributed to the organization's ability to come up with and implement so many improvements? And why had they resulted in such positive results? Our employees felt better and the customers got happier. We were able to do more with less, and as we improved our abilities, we gained more customers. It was a positive spiral.

A few months after I had left the company, I found out just how much the IT company had changed. From time to time I called Roger and asked him how things were going. During one of our conversations he enthusiastically told me that Eric, the managing director, had recently been convinced to replace almost every server with a more luxurious and allegedly better version. Roger was far from a technology fan and his enthusiasm surprised me at first, but I soon realized that it was not the high quality of the new server model he was so enthusiastic about. Strangely enough it was actually about the poor quality of the new servers. The servers had many small faults and strange problems that required a lot of adjustments. But because everyone at the IT company had become so used to identifying and solving problems in their everyday work, they had quickly been able to deal with the many small concerns caused by the big change. Everything had gone smoothly because a large number of small improvements supported the major change. Roger said that one of the company's main competitors had also been convinced by the marketing and bought the same kind of servers. However, the project had ended in total disaster for the competitor.

My telephone conversation with Roger made me understand another aspect of effective improvement work where everyone is involved. Not only does this lead to small problems being avoided on a day-to-day basis, it also creates flexibility and an ability to learn in an organization. It makes larger changes easier to handle, regardless of whether they are due to changes in the surrounding world or internal decisions. And that is not all, it struck me. Since all the small ideas and improvements are very hard to copy, effective improvement work can give a company competitive advantages that cannot be recreated by others. Anyone could buy new servers, but only the IT company could make them work so well, in such a short amount of time, using such a small amount of resources.

Talking to Roger got me thinking back to my time at the IT company. Why had we gotten things moving so quickly? Why had so many people chosen to take part, and why was almost no one against it? I sat down and produced my own list of the five most important reasons for the IT company's successful improvement work. I came up with the following five success factors:

1. Focus: clear targets
2. Visualization: highlighting positive results
3. Simplicity: tools that everyone can and wants to use
4. Ownership: to change rather than being changed
5. Systematic approach: clear game rules

Focus: Clear Targets

At the IT company we often wanted to do everything at once. So much should have been better and so much should have been different. But we worked hard to focus. We divided up, broke down, voted, simplified, and discarded. As a result we could limit ourselves to small and concrete areas we felt we could tackle and that were important to us who worked there.

It was like we were always working in a funnel. We started off with a large mass of unnecessary hassle and irritation that we divided into categories and prioritized through voting. By measuring and setting targets we focused the problem, and then we divided it into smaller parts using our fishbone diagrams. The smaller subproblems were in turn prioritized by voting and tackled one by one through the implementation of several small improvements.

Visualization: Highlighting Positive Results

Above all we wanted to create a positive atmosphere. We wanted to make everyone feel that we were successful and that we were doing good things. We also wanted to show how important improvements were. We did this by sharing examples of implemented improvements. We used every available communication channel. We even started to look for new ways of spreading information to make sure that no one could avoid it. Everyone was expected to attend the improvement meetings, and the results were visualized as improvement activities on the improvement boards. However, if anyone missed an improvement meeting and did not see what was on the improvement board, he or she would hopefully read the improvement letter that was sent by e-mail every month. We communicated information about improvement targets, regarding both improvement results and the number of implemented improvement activities, and when we achieved our targets, we organized improvement parties with an event that we started to call "improvement exhibitions." In these exhibitions every improvement group presented the improvement it was most proud of. We voted on each other's improvements and gave out improvement awards and improvement prizes to the improvement groups that received the most votes. The improvement prizes were often improvement trips, where the improvement group went on a study visit to another company that was also good at improvement work.

The positive atmosphere that was created had a side effect that we had not expected. We were suddenly able to speak more directly and in a less hostile way about the problems we had. We felt more confident and stopped blaming each other. Instead we looked at the situation as it was, using the facts that we had. Statements like these:

- This is not our fault.
- These figures are not right.
- We are doing the best we can.
- The manager won't like that.
- It's always been like that.

were replaced by questions such as:

- Why haven't we achieved our target?
- Why did things not turn out as planned?
- What are the reasons?
- What can we do about the problem?
- How can we make sure it does not happen again?

Simplicity: Tools That Everyone Can and Wants to Use

Maybe we did not know enough theory to make things complicated. Whatever the reason, we did the right thing when we chose the simple approach—this proved to work in the long term. It also led to benefits we had not expected. New employees did not need any special training to understand our improvement method. We did not need additional support resources to move forward. It only took a small amount of the managers' time, and instead of being involved in details and firefighting, they were able to focus on more important, more long-term issues, such as increasing staff competence in small, continuous steps.

The simplicity of our approach also meant that we progressed quickly and that everyone was able to contribute. Time was our most limited resource, and we could not afford not to use everyone's creativity.

A Huge Waste

At the IT company, we were reporting just over five small and simple implemented improvements (the activities written on the to-do list) per employee during the year I was working there. In Sweden the average was 0.48 improvements per person in 2007 (according to SIFV—Swedish Institute for Suggestion Systems). This is not even one improvement per employee every two years. However, surveys from companies in different sectors show that an implemented improvement is worth on average $150 to $250. What a huge waste!

All the methods and tools we used were simple, but our favorite remained the fishbone diagram. It rarely took more than 15 minutes to find good solutions to difficult problems. Everyone found it easy to take part and contribute, and even though not every suggestion could end up on the list of top priorities, everyone had been involved in deciding on how to tackle our problems. This meant that virtually everyone backed the solutions we agreed on. I even believe that some of my colleagues became just as fond of Post-its as I am.

Sometimes we felt it was negative to talk about problems all the time. Therefore we started to use the fishbone diagram to find the root causes of positive deviations as well. This helped us identify the behaviors that led to success. "Why is group X so good at achieving its targets?" or "Why is customer Y so satisfied" were examples of questions we asked to identify key behaviors for success. The rule used to be that the end justified the means, but once we had identified behaviors that led to success we started to follow up and encourage key behaviors instead of only focusing on the short-term results we wanted to achieve.

Ownership: To Change Rather Than Being Changed

When I was new at the IT company, I went around with Roger and talked with our colleagues. I was struck by just how much everyone knew about his or her individual area, how much energy people spent dealing with the obstacles they had, and how frustrated they were that things were going badly for the IT company. Their main worry was not about losing their jobs if the company were to go under or that their shares (the people who owned any) in the company would fall in value. They were more worried about doing a good job and contributing to something they felt was important and that they had already invested a part of their lives in. But if these individuals were so motivated and competent, why was the organization so ineffective and even destructive at times?

What was preventing our colleagues from making the most of their competence and creativity?

It came down simply to patterns, tradition, and habits. The managers at the IT company had learned that their job was to tell their employees what to do and then act the hero when any problems arose. Managers who did not know more than their colleagues were often looked down on. Managers therefore kept information to themselves and made sure that they developed their own competence first to make sure they were always ahead of their employees.

It was a large mental leap to go from micromanaging employees to giving them trust and responsibility to develop their own methods for achieving expected results. However, as time went by, managers went through the important change of "asking" rather than "telling."

Managers stopped presenting complicated reports, key figures, and action plans to their employees. Instead they started asking for fact-based reports on the current state, high-priority problem areas, and the reasons behind these problems. They also asked for updates on improvement activities that either had been implemented or were to be carried out. Every group was given a budget for its improvement work. Of course, managers still gave clear frameworks and expectations, and if an idea did not give any clear benefits or if it cost too much, it was not implemented.

- -

Brain or Hands—You Choose!

Henry Ford said something like, "Why is it every time I ask for a pair of hands, they come with a brain attached?" I can agree with him that people's desire to think and have control over their own lives makes the world more complex and difficult to handle. But you have only two alternatives as far as I can see. Either you try to prevent people from thinking for themselves, or you utilize their will to do so.

- -

Systematic Approach: Clear Game Rules

Roger spent quite a lot of time thinking about why people acted the way they did and why things turned out the way they did. During one of our telephone conversations after my time at the IT company, Roger told me he had been given the responsibility of showing visitors around because visitors had started to show greater interest in the IT company's work with continuous improvement than in bandwidths and backup frequencies. I suggested he had gotten the assignment because he was such a friendly and competent guy as well. Roger ignored my remark and instead shared one of his many thoughts with me. He told me about a comment an employee of one of the IT company's most important suppliers had made when he was showing a group around.

The supplier's employee said, "The atmosphere seems to have changed here. You appear to be having so much fun together. It must have something to do with all the company parties we saw photos of in your break room." Then he turned to his colleagues and said, "Maybe we should have a few more parties together to improve our atmosphere!"

Roger said that this comment had made him think. Was the atmosphere better at the IT company because they were partying together more often?

"I thought this was making things too simple," said Roger. "The atmosphere at a company cannot be improved in the long term simply by giving people more doughnuts during their Friday coffee break, having more frequent company parties, or doing more laps around the go-cart track together. There is nothing negative about partying in itself, but you don't take full advantage of it if you don't do it to celebrate joint successes that everyone has played a part in," he continued. "We have clear game rules making clear that everyone is expected and given a fair chance to contribute to our joint targets, and it's above all our joint successes and the visible result from our improvement work that has improved our atmosphere. Our celebrations have merely worked as a catalyst in this change toward a more positive atmosphere," Roger continued. "The visitor misinterpreted what he saw. He made the common mistake of only looking at the surface, instead of looking more deeply at the underlying causes. On the surface you see something that you could describe as a positive company culture, but underneath there is a clear and solid structure," Roger ended.

As always Roger had made me think, and I thought for quite a while after I had ended the call. Had we really had such clear game rules as Roger had said? Had we had a system? It took me some time to realize it, but he was definitely right. Of course we had had a system—it just had not been written down on paper with the heading "The IT company's improvement system." Maybe it was so simple and obvious that we did not need to write it down, but I thought it was about time to put it down in print.

> At the IT company we orienteer together to improve the entire flow by focusing on unnecessary hassle and the (internal) customer need. We visualize our positive results and use easy-to-use tools to ensure that everyone can and wants to take part.

Description of the IT company's systematic improvement work

Analysis of the Results

Imagine what would happen if I took you and ten of your colleagues to a junkyard and asked you to build whatever you wanted.

Think Inside the Box to Ignite the Creative Spark

The most common reaction would probably be to just stand there looking around, not sure what to do. You might see enterprising people starting to search through the clutter at random, but coordinated activities would be highly improbable. Imagine instead that I asked you to build a vehicle that could transport all of you at least ten yards without any of you touching the ground. Now your heads would probably fill with images of wheels, axles, planks to stand on, and steering wheels to guide you along the way. Instantly you would become more creative and could start to organize and divide the work among you. Some people think that creativity grows best when all boundaries are removed. At the IT company we found that the opposite was true. When we limited and clarified the task, it became easier for everyone to contribute.

Maximize Your Opportunities to Learn

At the IT company we sometimes discussed what to visualize. The answer came when we asked ourselves why we should visualize things at all. For us visualization was a tool for creating a positive atmosphere and conditions for continual learning. We experienced the truth in the statement "We learn from our mistakes." In successful organizations people talk about "treasuring your problems." In less successful organizations the approach is more about "sweeping problems under the rug." When you treasure your problems they become opportunities for learning and improvement. If you want to learn a lot, you want to find a lot of problems to learn from. And if you want to find a lot of problems, you visualize your targets and standards in a way that enables you to constantly check your current state against them. Problems are then visualized as they occur, and that presents a perfect opportunity to learn and improve.

Make It Easy to Do Right, Difficult to Do Wrong

When I joined, the IT company was a place where it was easy to make mistakes. It was unclear what had to be achieved and how everyone could contribute. If expectations are not clearly set out, the logical result is that they will not be met. Disappointment and irritation will follow soon after. But people with high ambitions do not only clarify their expectations. They also work out how to make it easy to do right and difficult to do wrong. If you want short meetings, you take the chairs away. If you want to avoid paper and cups being left on work surfaces and counters, you use sloping surfaces where it will be impossible to leave things.

If you cannot work out how to make the right behavior easy, you can look for a solution that makes it fun to do the right thing. "Fun to do right" is a very good substitute for "easy to do right."

Successful Improvement Leadership

At the IT company, *coaching* was a popular word. "We need to be better at coaching each other," was a statement you might hear during a meeting when things had not turned out as planned. However, you could often hear managers scolding employees who had made a mistake and hear managers telling their employees exactly how to solve their problems. Despite the fact that it did not result in greater commitment or improve anyone's performance, this seemed to reflect the most common leadership approach at the company.

"I've told them so many times how to do their jobs, but they still persist in finding their own methods. Although they don't understand how everything fits together, they insist on fiddling with the details and messing things up." This is something I remember overhearing Jonny, the operations manager, saying during a coffee break in my first month at the IT company.

When I was still new at the IT company, I often heard managers and employees arguing about different things—the right to take a break, how long the break should be, whether they could take their cups to their workstation, and what time they should arrive at work in the morning. They seemed to take every opportunity to have an argument. The relationship between managers and employees seemed to be more about conflict and power struggles than about how to collaborate and achieve something together.

Roger and I definitely saw potential in coaching each other at the IT company—the problem was that the managers at the IT company had never agreed on what a coaching approach meant in practice. At a management team meeting a few months before the end of my year at the IT company, a few managers started questioning whether there really was any major value in every improvement that the groups of the organization had made. Roger and I saw this as an opportunity. We suggested that the next management team meeting should focus on the question, "How can we get even more out of the groups' improvement work?"

At the meeting one month later Roger took command directly. He was worried that there would be merely an unstructured discussion on how to get more out of the organization's improvement work, so he started by asking everyone to give a mark from zero to 10 for the statement "We are good enough at coaching our colleagues in their improvement work." The statement was already on the flipchart, and everyone was asked to put his or her individual mark on a Post-it note.

"You have 30 seconds to write your answer on the Post-it note and put it on the scale," said Roger. Someone asked if they should answer based on their own department or based on the company as a whole. Roger said that either was fine.

Once all the notes had been added to the scale, I put a blue line where the average mark was.

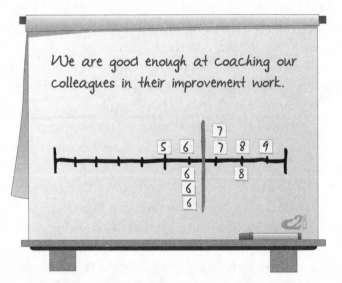

Current state analysis of the managers' ability to coach

"All right," I said. "Today we are approximately at 6.5. So there is potential for us to be better. If we use this as our starting point for working together to improve our coaching ability over the next six months and then do this survey again, what score do you think would be reasonable?"

"To have gone one step further up the scale," suggested finance manager Lena cautiously.

"Come on! Surely we can aim for 9," said Peter, the purchasing manager.

No one protested.

"Do you remember how we define an improvement?" asked Roger. "A solved problem. And a problem is the gap between where we are now and where we want to be," he said without waiting for anyone to answer.

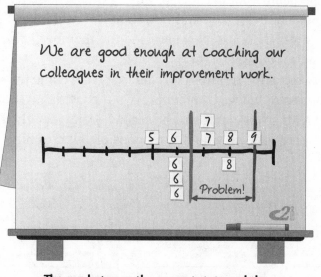

**The gap between the current state and the
target is the problem to solve**

"Now, let's analyze the problem we are facing," I said, while Roger put the fishbone guide on the wall.

Formulate the question: Focus the problem using a "Why" question   1 minute

Individual work: Answer the question on Post-it notes (one reply per note)   3 minutes

Spread out the notes: Group the notes and give the branches headings   5 minutes

Have consensus through voting: Prioritize the root cause groups (branches)   1 minute

Your to-do list: List solutions and the person responsible, including completion date   5 minutes

Simple instructions for producing a fishbone diagram in 15 minutes

We divided the managers into two groups, and Roger and I each took responsibility for one group. During the work we talked about the purpose of each step and how long it would take. When the group had finished a step, we praised the members' work before moving on to the next step.

The two groups reported on what they had come up with. The first group said that we could improve our coaching if the purpose of our coaching was clarified. The second group thought that it was important to agree on who was responsible for coaching whom.

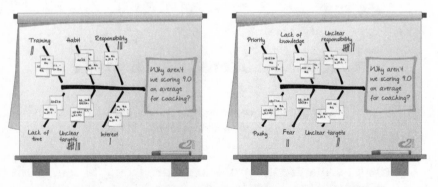

The two completed fishbone diagrams. "Unclear responsibility" and "Unclear targets" were considered to be the most important root causes respectively.

We had a short discussion on the groups' suggestions. We agreed that the first thing we needed to do was to help all improvement groups set targets based on the overall objectives of the company. The main purpose of coaching was to support the group or groups of employees the managers were responsible for in identifying and carrying out the activities demanded by the situation to reach a target. This also addressed the issue put forward by the second manager group. Every manager would coach the groups he or she was responsible for in the organization, while the managing director would coach the members of the management team.

When we had completed the fishbone exercise by documenting our proposed improvements, Roger asked the group members what they thought his and my role had been during the meeting. After a short silence, Eric said, "You've been our coaches."

"Exactly," said Roger, who could not hide his delight at the surprise in Eric's voice. "We have been your coaches, and now we want your feedback. Talk to the person sitting next to you about what was good about our way of coaching and what could have been done better." We gave them three minutes, and afterward we summarized their thoughts on the flipchart.

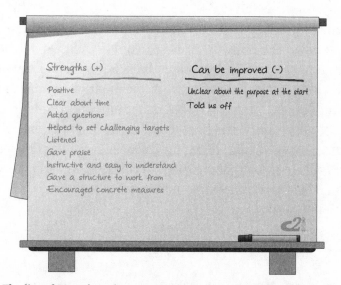

The list of Roger's and my strengths and weaknesses as coaches

To our joy, Stefan, the sales manager, helped us to summarize the whole point of our exercise: "This is a really important piece of paper. If we can be clear about our purpose and avoid telling people off, we have the perfect recipe for successful coaching there in the left column."

Jonny then added the finishing touch: "Yes, maybe we should try to shut up a little more often and listen to what people are saying," he admitted with a smile. This ended the day's meeting.

Interested or Interesting?

How many questions do you ask compared with the number of statements you make? What is your question-statement ratio? Do you try to be more interested or more interesting? If you double your question-statement ratio, I am convinced that you will both learn more and get more out of your colleagues.

How a Six-Legged Spider Helped Us Become Better Coaches

"Joakim, do you have half an hour?" I heard someone asking as I walked down the hallway. At first I couldn't tell where the voice had come from, but when I walked back a few steps I saw Jonny's head sticking out of Eric's office. A few months had passed since our management meeting about coaching, and I only had a few weeks left of my one-year fixed term at the IT company.

"Sure, Jonny," I said, entering the office and nodding hello to Eric, who sat in a chair facing the wall where a large flipchart paper was hung. On the paper was something that looked like a giant spider with text around it.

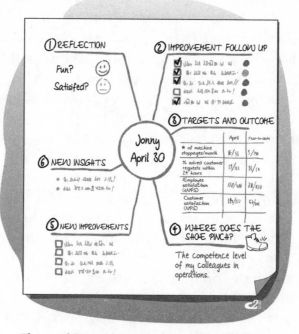

**The coaching spider Jonny had prepared before
getting his coaching from Eric**

"We would like you to sit here and listen while I get some coaching from Eric," Jonny told me. "You will get to ask questions at the end, but you have to keep quiet until we're done," he added. I took a chair and sat down.

Jonny went up to the large paper on the wall and started talking. At the same time I saw Eric pushing a button on his phone. Jonny began by saying that he had had fun in the last month and that he was fairly satisfied with his own contribution. Next Jonny reviewed his list of improvements and his outcome toward his targets. On the flipchart paper, successfully implemented improvements were followed by a green dot, improvements that had not been implemented according to plan were followed by a red dot, and improvements that Jonny had implemented with a result that was not to his satisfaction were followed by an orange dot. When Jonny had achieved a target, he had written the outcome in green, and when he had not achieved a target, it was written in red. All of this made it a lot easier for me grasp Jonny's situation. Next Jonny turned to the leg in the spider with the title "Where does the shoe pinch?" Jonny started talking but stopped in the middle of a sentence. "I realize that the words I have written here aren't entirely correct," he admitted after a short pause. "After having gone through my status once again I see that the true cause of my challenges is more about my own ability to be clear about what I expect from my colleagues rather than their competence level." Jonny picked up a pen to modify both his answer regarding the shoe pinch and a couple of the improvements under the fifth leg in his spider. When he was done, he finished his monologue by telling Eric about the improvements he was going to implement to get an even better outcome next month and what he had learned the previous month.

The whole time Jonny spoke both Eric and I sat completely quiet. I could not help being amazed. I had never thought I would be able to learn so much about Jonny and the challenges he faced in his organization. Now I had in less than 10 minutes. When Jonny became silent, Eric started talking. He commented on the progress Jonny had made during the last month and said that he was impressed by how honest Jonny was when facing his challenges. Then Eric asked Jonny a few questions about what had prevented Jonny from implementing all planned improvements and why he had not gotten the result he had expected from all of them.

Finding the Best Conductors of Change

Physicists must make good conductors of change, because you will find the best definition of a conductor in physics books: "A conductor is a body that transfers light, energy, and heat." It is so simple and obvious. Conductors of change convey light so that we can see where we are going—our targets. They give us energy through competence so that we are able to do what needs to be done, and they provide heat through encouragement, praise, and motivation to enable us to keep on going.

During the rest of the coaching session Eric addressed the shoe pinch from different angles. It seemed to me that he was eager to make sure he had completely understood where Jonny's shoe pinched. After a while, when they both became silent, Eric suggested that they should evaluate the coaching session. Jonny agreed, but then something strange happened. It looked like they were going to play rock-paper-scissors, but instead of making a rock, paper, or scissors with their hands, both of them held out a number of fingers simultaneously. They did it two times, and the first time Eric held out four fingers and Jonny three and the second time both of them held out five fingers.

"What was that?" I could not help asking despite my instructions to keep quiet.

"You should know. It's basically your own concept," Jonny said with a proud grin on his face. "You and Roger always nag us about the importance of evaluating everything we do, and I don't know how many times I've heard you say that we should 'keep it simple.' What you just saw is our simple coaching session evaluation," he finished.

"First we give a mark from one to five for how we felt during the coaching, and then we give a mark from one to five for how we feel about the specified way forward. If we feel that our communication is open and honest we give a high mark the first round, and if we believe the specified improvements will take us where we want to go we give a high mark the second round," Eric clarified.

"Brilliant," I said, feeling both proud and impressed. "There are a few other things I need you to explain to me, though. First of all, how did you come up with this?" I asked.

"The two of us started developing this concept of result-oriented coaching immediately after the management meeting when you and Roger coached us. At the meeting we decided that the purpose of coaching is to support each other in achieving our targets and that I as managing director am the head coach of the management team. This way of coaching is our way of turning those decisions into reality," Eric explained.

"The other members of the management team should get some credit for supporting the development of the coaching concept as well," said Jonny. "To Stefan it was important that we didn't get too result oriented. That's why we start with if we have had fun and if we feel satisfied with our own efforts. Roger, of course, gave the concept its orienteering touch. He helped us put emphasis on where we are in relation to our targets, whether we have made the expected progress, and what is preventing us from closing the gaps. Lena introduced the idea of "silent coaching" and made Eric agree to being silent during the first 10 minutes of each coaching session," he added.

"So that was what you were doing with your phone. You started a timer, right?" I asked.

Eric nodded with a smile. "I didn't think I would have any problems listening without jumping in to give advice, but setting the timer has really helped me a lot," he confessed.

"That idea has truly turned out better than I expected," Jonny admitted. "Calling it silent coaching is really accurate. To be given the opportunity to talk freely in front of what could be considered a witness is powerful. The coaching session we just had is not the first time, and will for sure not be the last, when I come to important realizations when listening to myself talking."

"And that was what happened before you changed what you had written about your shoe pinch?" I inquired.

"Exactly," Jonny replied. "I think the 10-minute rule gives time for both self-reflection and self-correction. Above all it allows you to find your own solutions to your problems, and I think that is a prerequisite for personal growth," he added, not able to hide his exhilaration. Hearing Jonny speak was like music to my ears. To be honest, he was the last person I had expected to hear say those words, but seeing how he had transformed himself as a leader made me feel great.

"There is another benefit to that rule," Eric said after having thought for a few seconds about what Jonny had just said. "It also gives me the chance to truly listen without my mind being occupied with trying to come up with solutions to problems other people are better suited to solve. I think I do more good as a coach if I focus on truly understanding the other person's situation. By listening and asking questions to understand the other person completely I help the person understand himself or herself better," he added, looking at Jonny, who nodded his confirmation.

"Do you just listen in general, or do you listen for anything in particular when you coach someone?" I asked Eric.

"I haven't thought about that, but now that you're asking I think I almost intuitively have listened for two things in particular," he started after a moment of thought. "First of all I listen to the tone of voice to evaluate the level of commitment and energy. If the person I am coaching is not committed to achieving his or her targets, we need to find and address the causes for that. The other thing I listen for is whether the person I am coaching gives a correct and honest description of his or her current state. If not, the planned improvements to progress toward the target will probably be of limited effect. Therefore I allow myself to ask a lot of challenging questions about the indicated shoe pinch," Eric finished, sounding like a true coaching expert.

For some reason I felt that I immediately had to learn everything there was to know about the coaching concept they had created. "How often do you coach everyone in the management team like this?" I continued my inquiry.

"I haven't actually started coaching everyone yet. This was the third time I coached Jonny, and I want to make sure he and the rest of the members of the management team get coaching once a month in the future. We still need to introduce Nadia to the concept, but no one has had any problem in adopting it so far. When you produce your first spider chart, you might not have any improvements to follow up on, but that's not a problem. When Jonny did his first spider he changed the title of that leg to 'Progress' and listed the activities that had taken him closer to his target during the month that had passed. Wasn't that what you did?" Eric asked, turning to Jonny.

"Yes, that's what I did," Jonny answered, "but I think you are forgetting another problem I had the first time you coached me.

Not only did I have a hard time reporting my status in relation to my targets, I was even a bit unsure of what my targets were."

"You are right, I forgot," Eric admitted. "But the coaching was all right anyway, don't you think?" he asked Jonny.

"Absolutely, the coaching was valuable anyway. The best thing to do is to get started and make improvements along the way. What's more, during the first coaching session I realized how to define my targets by involving my customers. My internal customers are my colleagues in the operations and customer support groups, and after talking to them I decided on two targets that would stimulate me to support the groups in their improvement work. I also decided to have targets for both internal and external customer satisfaction. I searched the Internet and found measurements called "Net Promoter Score" and "employee Net Promoter Score." Since then, each month I ask a few customers how likely they are to recommend our services to a friend or colleague and a few employees how likely they are to recommend that a friend start working for me on a scale from 1 to 10. I have divided our customers and the people working for me into groups to make sure everyone gets to answer the question at least once a year," Jonny said, amazing me with how far they had come in only a couple of months.

"I'm impressed," I said. "But Eric, are you sure you will have time to coach everyone in the management team every month?" I asked cautiously, afraid to find that it was all too good to be true.

"You don't have to worry," Eric responded with a calming smile. "We have thought about that, too. That's why we will introduce 'coaching in pairs' as soon as everyone has gotten started. In the future all of us in the management team will coach each other in pairs over breakfast before our monthly management meetings. It will only take an hour to receive and give coaching as long as our spiders are well prepared, and even though I hope that one or two will ask for my coaching in addition to the coaching in pairs it will definitely be a very effective method. "

"There are other benefits to that approach," Jonny chipped in. "Hopefully this way of coaching will replace those awful performance reviews where you are supposed to look back 12 months in time and prepare for another year of fumbling in the dark without continuous support," he began. "More important, it will be a great way of spreading improvements and insights between us and you too will get support and coaching like the rest of us," he quickly added, seeking Eric's approval since he probably felt that his first remark might have been a bit offensive to his boss.

"All of it is true," Eric agreed. "But the largest benefit is probably that all of us will become better coaches. The components of an improvement board are very similar to the components of our coaching spider, and if we bring these coaching principles and our improved coaching ability when we support our colleagues in their improvement work, we'll get even better results," he added with conviction.

"This investment will have the shortest payoff time ever," Jonny finished with a contagious laughter that rubbed off on me and Eric.

I left Eric's office confident that the IT company had a bright future.

One of the main reasons the IT company as a whole was able to change was because the managers worked together to change their attitude toward their colleagues and to improve their ability to coach. It did not happen overnight, but once the employees were given responsibility for achieving results and they were given good support, we saw changes that many of us had not thought were possible.

Analysis of the Leadership

It is important to set and break down targets in all sections of a company. It frees the power of being part of something bigger and shows all employees how their areas of responsibility contribute to the company as a whole. It does not have to be difficult, and when good targets have been formulated, it makes many other things easier. For example, clear targets help us work proactively; they show us where to focus our energy and what to talk about at meetings.

Do You Want to Play Catch?

One of the methods used for breaking down targets is called catchball. When company leaders use this technique, they begin by communicating what is important for the company (the overall objectives). Then they "throw the ball" to their colleagues, asking them to propose targets that they should work on to contribute to the company's overall objectives. The ball may need to be thrown back and forth a few times to make sure everyone involved is satisfied. Good targets are easy to follow up on—and the more often you check your progress toward your target, the more opportunities you get to interpret and learn from the results you achieve. This also means that the changes you need to make to stay on the right course toward your target are smaller and easier to implement.

Do Not Forget to Feed the Beast

One of the most important success factors in improvement work is management support. However, lack of commitment from higher management is not a valid excuse for improvement coaches and middle managers to avoid taking initiative. It is true that it is more difficult to achieve results if you do not have the full support of management, but it does not have to be a reason to give up. It is much better to see this as a sign that management needs support in its change process.

For a person, manager or not, to want to change, he or she needs to answer yes to the following questions: "Can I do it?" and "Is it worth it?" This is what Joseph Grenny and his coauthors say in the book *Influencer: The Power to Change Anything*. The book also shows that verbal argumentation is a highly overrated method when trying to convince a person of his or her ability and the potential advantages of working in a new way. Many of our actions are automatic—they are guided by our experiences and the presupposed ideas we have gained from these experiences. This means that coaches and leaders who want to influence behavior should primarily focus on creating new experiences. When the management team at the IT company experienced working with improvements in the same way as the other groups in the company, they realized the benefit of the approach and increased their understanding of how to support their colleagues in the improvement work.

Another kind of leader who is not committed to improvement work is a manager who is only interested in the results and not how the results are achieved. However, I have seen evidence that this does not have to be an obstacle either.

"I call this feeding the beast," an experienced improvement coach once told me. "There are key figures we are expected to report that we don't really see the purpose of. But we make sure we report the figures that the manager wants every month. It only takes a few minutes, and when it's done, we can carry on working with improvements according to the principles that we believe in."

Spreading the Continuous Improvement Culture

Getting the improvement work started at the IT company took a lot of time and required a lot of energy, and the company's improvement work was still far from being world-class when I finished my one-year contract. But a good foundation had been laid and the energy used had created results. These results motivated people, and the renewed energy could be invested in developing the improvement work even further.

As the IT company's reputation improved, the demand for the company's services increased. The attitude toward improvement work also changed from crisis resolution to growth strategy. The management team's ambition became to develop an approach that continuously stimulated improved results using fewer resources. This resulted in Roger and his colleagues in the management team making many changes that increased the pace and effectiveness of the company's improvement work after my time at the IT company.

A bit more than year after I had left I heard that one of the industry's giants had bought the IT company. I called Roger to meet him for a beer after work. Roger was as calm as always about the new changes.

"I'm sure everything will be fine. We'll probably have even more to do now, so at least none of us have to worry about losing our jobs," he answered when I asked what he thought about the acquisition. He also told me that he had already been asked to run a small department. This department was going to be responsible for developing and spreading improvement work throughout the now much larger company.

"Great! That'll be an amazing challenge," I said. "But I do have one question I really want to ask you. You could say that you're starting over from the beginning again—so what are you going to do to make sure it is even better this time?"

"I don't know if I'm going to do anything much differently," started Roger. "It is the journey and what you learn together along the way that is important. If you force people to follow perfect, ready-made solutions it gets more difficult to create involvement and encourage ownership. I've already decided to concentrate on three parts—momentum, direction, and structure. First we build momentum, and then we start adjusting our direction. We also need a structure that helps us keep up the pace and control the direction of the improvement work with a minimum amount of administration," said Roger just as two beers were put in front of us on the table.

"We build momentum by working together on concrete problems that are relevant to the employees. Then I think it is important to challenge everyone to think differently and to show them that it is about working smarter, not harder," Roger continued before pausing to take a sip of beer.

"It Is Stupid to Set Smart Targets"

The quote in this heading comes from a production manager with a wealth of experience in changing how people think. "We had been taught to set SMART targets: Specific, Measurable, Acceptable, Realistic, and Time-bound. But this isn't what we did—we used SMAST instead, because we set Senseless targets, not Realistic ones. If we set senseless, extremely challenging targets, we can't achieve them by simply sweating more. We are forced to think differently and find new, smarter solutions."

"At the IT company we introduced targets for the improvement process early on," Roger said. "We started to measure how many improvements each person made. This not only sped up the pace of the improvement work, it also helped us to see who needed support and where we as leaders should focus our efforts. We started to compare ourselves with other companies and kept on raising the bar. We considered 'Swedish top class' to be 7 improvements per person per year, 13 was 'European top class,' while 20 improvements per person per year was only achieved by the best in the world. As we started tracking the number of improvements we became better at sharing ideas and copying each other's improvements. We also gave employees more chances to decide for themselves which investments were important for the company. This led to quicker decisions and a lighter workload for our managers," Roger finished his answer.

"Is there really nothing you would do any differently?" I pressured on.

"Yes, there was one area we should have started to focus on a bit earlier at the IT company. The mistake made us lose some of the momentum we had built at the start. It might be a bit of a paradox, but what we lacked was clearer guidance from our managers. We began well by using simple methods to work on concrete problems. But when we had dealt with the most obvious problems, a few groups lost their drive. It took us a while to realize what was missing—but when we started to communicate and break down the company's overall objectives together, we got a tool that we could use to continually challenge ourselves to achieve better results. Connecting our improvement work to the company objectives helped maintain and even increase the pace of our improvement work. I think that everyone gained a lot of energy by seeing their own efforts in a wider context."

Roger's calmness and conviction impressed me. However, I seemed more excited than he was, and I found it difficult to hold back my concerns about how he would make it in his new role.

"I agree completely with what you say. But how are you going to manage all this in such a large company? I mean, sharing lessons and improvements effectively, guiding the improvement work toward the overall objectives, following up and increasing the effect of people's efforts by prioritizing where to focus your own and other managers' coaching—there's a lot to keep track of!"

Roger smiled.

"You're right—there is a lot to keep track of! But that was already the case when I only had 100 colleagues—and it would have been the same if there had been even fewer of us. This is why my third component is to create a structure that makes the work easier. Two important features of this structure are our 'board meetings' and our simple approach for setting targets and coaching each other to achieve them. And as you know we've been using an electronic system for a long time now that keeps track of all improvements at the IT company. This has made it easier to follow up on our improvement activities and communicate the good examples between groups and departments. The documentation and classification of all our improvements have also given us a fact base for further improvement, both in the business and in our improvement process. Together our electronic support system, our 'board meetings,' and the way we set targets and coach each other have given us a solid foundation for successful improvement work," said Roger reassuringly.

Before we went our separate ways, I remembered that I had forgotten to ask Roger something.

"Roger, how many improvements have you guys made per person so far this year?" I asked.

"Our most recent statistics show an annual rate of more than 20 improvements per person. But now that we've been acquired our average number of completed improvements per person has fallen dramatically. We just need to start on a new journey toward becoming the best in the world!" ended Roger.

Best in the world

Analysis of Spreading the Culture

Why should you set targets for and measure the number of improvements? It is all about putting focus on and developing one of the most important processes in a company. If this process improves, so does the company's ability to learn.

Quantity Drives Quality

What other abilities are more important for the long-term survival of your company? To make improvement and learning part of your day-to-day work, you need to measure and follow them up. A good figure to measure is the number of implemented improvements per employee, as this stimulates small improvements that are easy to implement rather than large projects that need a lot of time and resources. To measure like this is also recommended in research, no matter if it is large or small improvements you want. In his book *Cracking Creativity*, Michael Michalko states that researchers have been trying for centuries to identify what makes a person creative. What qualities do people with the best ideas have? Can we list the three most important qualities they have in common? No, we can't. Despite persistent attempts, researchers have only been able to show a connection to one single factor. People who have the best ideas are the people who have the most ideas. Nothing else seems to matter. The only thing that drives the quality of your ideas is the number of ideas you have. Focusing on the number of improvement ideas through clear targets and frequent follow-up is therefore the method recommended by researchers to find the best ideas.

The way that some companies set and follow up targets pushes employees to work harder from year to year. These targets include number of quality deviations, delivery precision, costs, and so on. But these targets do not measure how good the company is at developing its ability to achieve more challenging targets in the future. One way of doing this is to also include targets that measure the extent of activity in the improvement work. Employees are then encouraged to work smarter rather than harder.

Getting Everyone Moving

Imagine that you are sitting behind the steering wheel of a large vehicle—for example, a bus—that is not moving. If you try to turn the wheel, you will find that it is heavy—the larger the vehicle, the more difficult it is to turn the steering wheel when the vehicle is not moving. However, if you put your foot on the accelerator and get the bus moving, it is quite easy to turn the steering wheel and guide it in the direction you want to go. You need to have momentum before you can start to steer. The same is true for improvement work.

"To start with, you have to get everyone moving—we can guide what direction they are moving in later on." This is what an insightful improvement coach told me when we met for the first time. The company he worked for had several hundred employees, and they are now among the best in Europe at improvement work (more than 13 improvements implemented per employee per year).

Starting Your Journey Toward Being the Best in the World (Practical Section)

Improvement meetings (or "board meetings" as we called them at the IT company) are an essential part of improvement work. These meetings preferably include three to eight people and last for a maximum of 30 minutes, and during this time you and your colleagues ask the four orienteering questions. Imagine that you have one meeting a week, and every meeting results in a number of implemented improvements equal to half the number of people at the meeting. This means that after 40 working weeks, you will have achieved 20 improvements per person. With this simple calculation I challenge you to join the best in the world in improvement work!

Where Are We?

It is normal to want to do everything all at once. But the best way to start is to choose one area to focus your improvement work on. One good way of doing this is to give everyone at the meeting Post-it notes and then ask them to write down all the unnecessary hassle that gets in their way in their daily work on separate notes. Collect all the notes, sort them into groups, and then vote on the unnecessary hassle that you, as a group, want to work on first. Remember to focus on something that you can influence yourselves. When you have chosen a hassle, you go on to measure the extent of the problem, if possible immediately, and visualize it on your board.

Another way of finding an improvement area is to answer the questions in the current state analysis in the next chapter and then choose the question with the lowest average score.

Where Are We Going?

You need to set a target to show everyone where you are going. How much can you reduce the amount of unnecessary hassle? How much can you increase the average score for the question? Visualize the target on your board.

How Are We Going to Get There?

Remember that a problem is the gap between where you are and where you want to be. Analyze the problem using a fishbone diagram and visualize your improvements on your board.

Formulate the question: Focus the problem using a "Why" question   1 minute

Individual work: Answer the question on Post-it notes (one reply per note)   8 minutes

Spread out the notes: Group the notes and give the branches headings   5 minutes

Have consensus through voting: Prioritize the root cause groups (branches)   1 minute

Your to-do list: List solutions and the person responsible, including completion date   5 minutes

Instructions for producing a fishbone diagram

It is a good idea to produce a fishbone diagram at each meeting, but it is not essential. Sometimes you can just look at the branch that was second in the list of priorities (the one that received the second highest number of votes) to help you find new, important improvements.

How Do We Make It All the Way to the Target?

Decide on how you are going to celebrate when you reach your final target. You also need to decide when you expect to get there. If you do not get there on time, ask yourselves why. You then have two choices. Either give yourself more time or focus your energy on something else. Also break down the final target into subtargets and decide when you will reach these subtargets and how you will celebrate when you get there. An alternative to celebrating an achieved outcome is to celebrate when you have made a specific number of improvements. Follow up at future meetings on where you are in relation to your targets and do not forget to celebrate and visualize your positive results along the way.

Current State Analysis of Your Improvement Work

If you want to improve your improvement work, this current state analysis is a perfect way to start. Fill out the self-assessment survey individually and calculate the average score for each question. Focus on the question with the lowest average score and apply the method described in the previous chapter.

1. Where we work, everyone is fully aware of why we need to work with improvements.

   No, not at all   **0 1 2 3 4 5 6 7 8 9 10**   *Yes, really*

2. Where we work, everyone can continually see how their own efforts contribute to the overall results of the company.

   No, not at all   **0 1 2 3 4 5 6 7 8 9 10**   *Yes, really*

3. Where we work, everyone is fully aware of how we should be working with improvements.

   No, not at all   **0 1 2 3 4 5 6 7 8 9 10**   *Yes, really*

4. Our improvement work is based on problems identified by the employees themselves.

   No, not at all   **0 1 2 3 4 5 6 7 8 9 10**   *Yes, really*

5. Where we work, the employees in all our work flows know what is considered value adding from the (internal) customer perspective.

   No, not at all   **0 1 2 3 4 5 6 7 8 9 10**   *Yes, really*

6. The way we work with improvements stimulates collaboration.

No, not at all **0 1 2 3 4 5 6 7 8 9 10** *Yes, really*

7. We gather facts to identify problems and the extent of these problems.

No, not at all **0 1 2 3 4 5 6 7 8 9 10** *Yes, really*

8. Decisions made in our organization are based on a true picture of our actual current state.

No, not at all **0 1 2 3 4 5 6 7 8 9 10** *Yes, really*

9. Where we work, everyone knows why we implement the improvements we do.

No, not at all **0 1 2 3 4 5 6 7 8 9 10** *Yes, really*

10. Our to-do lists include the person responsible and a completion date to ensure that we progress in our work.

No, not at all **0 1 2 3 4 5 6 7 8 9 10** *Yes, really*

11. We celebrate our successes frequently enough on our journey toward our targets.

No, not at all **0 1 2 3 4 5 6 7 8 9 10** *Yes, really*

12. We set targets and follow up our improvement work in a way that helps us to evaluate and improve our improvement work.

No, not at all **0 1 2 3 4 5 6 7 8 9 10** *Yes, really*

13. Our improvement work is focused on the overall objectives of the company.

No, not at all **0 1 2 3 4 5 6 7 8 9 10** *Yes, really*

14. We talk often enough about positive examples of improvements.

No, not at all **0 1 2 3 4 5 6 7 8 9 10** *Yes, really*

15. We always identify the root causes of our problems.

No, not at all **0 1 2 3 4 5 6 7 8 9 10** *Yes, really*

16. We have a sufficiently high level of participation in our improvement work.

No, not at all **0 1 2 3 4 5 6 7 8 9 10** *Yes, really*

17. Where we work, everyone feels a personal responsibility for developing his or her working methods.

No, not at all **0 1 2 3 4 5 6 7 8 9 10** *Yes, really*

18. Where we work, everyone knows what is expected from him or her in the improvement work.

No, not at all **0 1 2 3 4 5 6 7 8 9 10** *Yes, really*

19. My manager is sufficiently committed to improvement work.

No, not at all **0 1 2 3 4 5 6 7 8 9 10** *Yes, really*

20. We are good enough at coaching each other on our journey toward the targets.

No, not at all **0 1 2 3 4 5 6 7 8 9 10** *Yes, really*

Sustaining the Continuous Improvement Culture and the Five Cultural Pitfalls Preventing You from Succeeding

"So what's your secret?" I asked.

"What makes you think there is a secret?" Roger answered with a secretive smile.

Almost five years had passed since our time together at the IT company. We had kept in touch, though sporadically, and I had never stopped considering Roger my main mentor. It was evening and we had just been served our main course. The restaurant was Italian and trendy. The dinner was my initiative. I had used the fifth anniversary of our last unified success as an excuse, but to be honest I had something else in mind. I wanted to know Roger's secret. Over the last months I had seen Roger's face in different magazines more often than I had seen my own face in the mirror. At least it felt like it. I may read a lot of management magazines, but he was just unbelievably popular at the moment. I was of course aware of the success Roger had had at the IT giant after its acquisition of the IT company. It only took him a couple of years to turn it into a virtual improvement machine that appeared to develop and grow bigger every day. Since then he had started his own business as a continuous improvement consultant, and though his success hadn't evaded me the extent of it apparently had. According to the articles I had read his track record was flawless. Everything he did turned out better than expected, and in just a few years he had become the main authority on improvement work in the country. I thought it was time for him to teach me his success formula.

"Don't you try to deny it," I told him. "If you didn't have a secret recipe for success, you wouldn't be able to produce the results you do. So stop fooling around and share your guru secret," I continued, trying to provoke the practical Roger who I knew would dislike being called a management guru.

"I only do what we did together at the IT company. The basic principles of successful improvement work we had as a foundation there have stood the test of time. They are incredibly powerful in their simplicity and can help any organization progress on its continuous improvement journey," Roger answered.

"Oh no, you won't get away that easily!" I objected. "My work might not be known to the public, but at least you know that I have supported lots of organizations as a consultant, too. And sure, I have a lot of success stories, but sometimes the results have been mediocre compared to what we achieved at the IT company, and on a couple of occasions, to be completely truthful, the results completely failed to arrive. So, out with it! What have you done to become mister 100 percent?" I pressured on, but Roger was saved by the waiter, who topped off our wine glasses and took our dessert order.

When the waiter had left, I stared resolutely at Roger. "One hundred percent might be a bit of an exaggeration, but yes, things have been going quite well," Roger started slowly. I kept quiet, waiting for him to continue. "And, yes, I do have a little something that not many people working with continuous improvement know of," he went on after what seemed like an eternity. I exhaled and let my shoulders down, relieved that I hadn't been mistaken. "Before I let you know my secret, though, I want you to give me your perspective on what we did together at the IT company," Roger demanded. His promise to tell me his secret was more than enough for me to fulfill his wish.

"In short, you could say that we introduced a focused and systematic way of working with improvements and that we equipped our colleagues with a few effective and easy-to-use tools," I suggested confidently. I had to wait both for Roger's reaction and for his reply. It was obvious that he was trying to put words to a thought.

"In a way you are absolutely right, but from a different perspective that's an extreme simplification," he finally said. "In fact, to me that way of putting it is a great depreciation of what we actually achieved." Roger's objection made me both surprised and curious.

"Tell me more," I requested as we got our dessert.

"I agree that we were practical in our approach, but what we actually did was shift the mindsets of all the people working there. In other words, you could say that we acted our way into a new way of thinking rather than thought our way into a new way of acting at the IT company. We might not have been aware of it then, but if you ask me what we did at the IT company, I'd say we made a fundamental change in the corporate culture," Roger said emphatically. "The process of changing an organizational culture is hard to grasp. The change is a gradual evolution rather than a stepwise process, and the effect of a single action might be impossible to see. I've learned that it is quite common to be constantly questioning your efforts and doubting your success until one day when you suddenly realize that you have broken through," he continued.

"All right," I said to give myself some time to think. "You are telling me there is an important difference between changing a culture and introducing a set of tools," I started off, looking at Roger, who gave me an approving nod. "And if you do not understand that you are engaged in a cultural change and approach it as introducing a new tool, you won't reap the full benefits. It would be like giving someone a hammer instead of creating a wholehearted passion for hitting nails," I continued, eyes fixed on Roger, who nodded once again and smiled at my analogy.

I sat quiet for a while and then asked, "So, if a cultural change is abstract and hard to grasp, how can we tell if we succeed?"

"The best method is to listen for changes in the way people talk. At the IT company I got my first realization about our ongoing cultural change when I heard our colleagues talking about what to do about a problem together instead of putting blame on each other or a different department," Roger replied. "I noticed that we

eventually developed a completely new way of talking about ourselves, our situation, and our possibilities of creating the future we
desired. Our new way of addressing and solving problems together
and our way of working to continuously improve our business
became 'the way we do things around here.' On a more fundamental level we had actually changed 'the way we think around here,'
but when something becomes 'the way we think around here,' it
changes from being something observable to something invisible.

"Culture to a person is like water to a fish, you know," Roger
continued and then added, "Since you can't see it you are unaware
of it, but if it changes, you can be affected in dramatic ways."

The Five Cultural Pitfalls and How to Benefit from Roger's Secret

Both of us took a few bites of dessert.

"What is the first question?" Roger asked after a while. The
answer was so obvious I didn't know if he really expected an answer.

"Where are we?" I quickly replied when I noticed in his eyes
that he wanted me to say it.

"Exactly, and when you know the characteristics of corporate
culture you realize that that question is hard to answer from a cultural perspective. It could actually be that a culture misfortunate
for continuous improvement evolves without the people in the organization noticing. I call that falling into a cultural pitfall," Roger
said, and he withdrew a pen to write five lines on a paper napkin:

1. The Low-Hanging Fruit Trap
2. The Reality Illusion
3. The Emperor's New Clothes
4. The Efficiency Paradox
5. The Friendship Fallacy

"Is this supposed to be your secret?" I asked, looking suspi-
ciously at the napkin. Roger nodded. "But this means nothing to

me. I might have heard about that fruit trap, but apart from that this is pure gibberish," I complained.

"Have you ever thought about the power of language?" Roger asked.

"What power of language?" I answered impatiently, unable to see the point of Roger's question.

"Well, I wonder if you have thought about why we have concepts to begin with," Roger clarified. I decided to take Roger's question seriously. Thinking about it, I took a sip of wine.

"Of course!" I almost yelled. Roger, who saw the aha moment, couldn't suppress a smile.

"Share your thoughts," he said.

"Around Christmas the year after I had moved away from home my parents took me and my brother out for dinner," I began. "Before dinner we had a wine tasting, something I had never experienced before. We got four glasses of red wine and a piece of paper where we were supposed to write what tastes we could find in the different wines. I felt a bit awkward because sour was the best taste description I could give to all the wines, but when the sommelier had explained what kinds of tastes we could look for in the wines it was like their tastes changed. When I got concepts such as fruitiness, spiciness, and oak, I could start distinguishing them in the wines. After practicing some I even learned to tell what fruits, herbs, or spices the wines had hints of. That experience illustrates a general principle. Until you have a concept of something you won't be able to distinguish and relate to it in a good way," I finished, feeling elevated.

"Exactly," Roger confirmed. "The characteristics of an organizational culture—something abstract that changes gradually—are the main cause for organizations on continuous improvement journeys to get caught in these pitfalls. Since changes in culture are hard to see you, will also have difficulties seeing if your culture evolves in the wrong direction. To make matters worse, culture being as water to a fish, it is quite common to be stuck in one or more of these pitfalls without realizing it. But when these five concepts mean something to you, you will be able to distinguish behavior related to these five common cultural pitfalls and determine whether your organization is stuck in one of them or not. In other words your answer to where you are will be more accurate, and with that the activities you decide to implement to advance toward your goal will have much greater effect. In fact, I've seen many organizations that experience setbacks and waning employee commitment on their continuous improvement journeys deciding to 'restart' their initiative. Unfortunately, repeating what they did when they started will most probably, possibly after a short boost in commitment, take them back to the very place they want to leave. If they want to get out of the repetitive and energy-draining pattern, they need to take a closer look at their answer to the question about where they are. Hopefully that will make them realize that they are not at the starting point and that 'restarting' is impossible," Roger finished his long monologue.

I thought for a while about what Roger had said and then asked, "But wouldn't you say that it is a good ambition to try to reconnect with the basic principles of successful improvement work?"

"Definitely," Roger answered. "That is the right ambition, but if you don't get what you want, doing more of the same can't be the solution. Instead you should ask yourself what went wrong and which of the basic principles you need to approach differently or put greater stress on," Roger clarified.

"And that is what you will be able to do if you learn to recognize the five pitfalls?" I asked, being quite sure of the answer.

"You are right," Roger said, leaning back to allow the waiter to remove his plate. "But the main benefit of being aware of the cultural pitfalls is that it helps you avoid falling into one in the first place," he pointed out.

"Of course," I said. "But if you encounter an organization that has reason to believe that it has already fallen into a pitfall—let's say managers feel that they are doing everything according to the book but still don't get the results they expect—how do you help them?" I asked.

"First of all I let them know there's no reason to despair and remind them about the opportunity to learn from mistakes and that a challenge handled the right way will only make them stronger.

An organization that approaches the pitfall concept with openness and honesty will increase managers' insight about their current state, and those organizations will come out of any pitfall both stronger and wiser," Roger began his answer. "I also let them know that you don't pass the five pitfalls in a sequence and that they might find themselves stuck in more than one at a time. This is important to know since seen from the bottom a few pitfalls may even appear similar, but the causes for ending up in them are what distinguish them from one another. Thus the method for getting out of each pitfall is also unique. The rest of what I do to help is mostly about creating insight about their current state by describing the most common characteristics of each pitfall."

"But you don't just describe the pitfalls, right? You give them advice on how to get out as well, don't you?" I asked, letting it shine through that I was expecting more than just a description.

"Well yes, since I've encountered quite a few organizations stuck in a pitfall over the years I've learned what works if you want to get out," Roger admitted. "But, though the practical advice I give them might drastically improve their chances of getting out, I don't consider it being the important part. Changing culture is not as much about what you do as about how you are when you do it. You should also remember that cultural issues are about our thinking and feelings, and that can be sensitive stuff. What I provide is a defused way to approach these quite elusive topics, and I consider the reflection and discussion that takes place when I ask people where they are in relation to each pitfall to be the most important. Asking them not only to tell if they are in a pitfall but to specify where they are in relation to each pitfall, I encourage them to be precise in their thinking. That gives them deeper insight, which in turn helps them avoid pitfalls they haven't yet fallen into and makes the countermeasures they decide on more potent," Roger said with conviction.

"All right, now I know how to use my knowledge about the pitfalls. It is time for you teach me all about them," I requested. "By the way, imagine I am a manager, a management team, or a workgroup on one of your assignments and present it the way you would to them," I modified my request. I could tell Roger was ready to

share his secret. While he ordered two cups of coffee I took out a
pen and a notepad from my bag.

The Low-Hanging Fruit Trap

The Low-Hanging Fruit Trap is a very common pitfall during the
first phase of a continuous improvement journey. The improvement
potential is more obvious at the point in time when you start focusing on improvements. The low-hanging fruit is ripe, easy to reach,
and ready to be picked. This fact presents a great opportunity to
lay the foundation for a sustainable process of continuous improvement. It is in fact the best chance you will get to create commitment
around the tools and structures you introduce since they will most
probably create immediate and visible results. Experiencing positive results gives new energy, and this energy can be used to foster
a systematic approach that helps you build the improvement competence of your organization.

The initially obvious low-hanging fruit is also a potential threat
to your long-term success. Picking low-hanging fruit in a random
and sporadic manner produces results, but it does not build the
competence of the organization and it does not produce habits of
working together systematically to improve. The organizations
that do not use the energy from early successes to introduce a
structured approach based on distributed competence and decision making fall into the Low-Hanging Fruit Trap.

Where Are You?

If you have experienced a tsunami of improvement ideas, out of
which a large part were implemented, followed by a wave, followed
by a splash, followed by silence, you are probably caught in this
pitfall. The pattern of continuously smaller bumps in the development curve is common in several pitfalls, but if it is the result of
repeated idea campaigns with varying focus you can be sure you
have fallen into the Low-Hanging Fruit Trap.

Where are you and your colleagues?

How to Get Out

At the surface this problem might be perceived as a bad choice of method, but if you dig deeper you are likely to encounter an underlying fear of truly letting go of power and control. Some managers create a false sense of security for themselves by centralizing decisions and making sure they have an information and competence advantage over their colleagues. When the managers of the IT company began letting go of their need for control we got the opportunity to catalyze a change in mindsets by introducing new tool sets. Our early successes gave us energy and buy-in that we could invest in working systematically to spread our straightforward approach, get everyone on board, and create an improvement competent organization. Eventually our efforts resulted in a cultural shift.

Realizing that you are stuck in this pitfall is no reason to lose heart. You will soon get a new chance to succeed. If you do not work with improvements systematically, a great and obvious need for improvements will emerge sooner than you think. But to avoid creating an even bigger pitfall for yourself you need to understand that you do not need more of the same. You need something new, and this something should have the purpose of creating an improvement competent organization.

Idea Campaigns Kill Creativity!

Running an idea campaign is a popular method for tapping into the creativity of an organization. There is only one problem with them. They kill creativity! If there is an unmet need to be listened to in an organization, an idea campaign might create a surge of ideas, a surge so big that only a fraction of all ideas can be implemented. This means the majority of people will get yet another confirmation that no one listens to their ideas, and next time they are less likely to contribute.

Getting out of the Low-Hanging Fruit Trap requires the willingness to let go of control and distribute both decision-making power and ability in the organization. The rest is a two-step process. Just as we did at the IT company, you first need to make sure that all teams of your organization are equipped with simple methods to work on concrete problems and the time to do so systematically together. The second step, which came a bit too late at the IT company, is to create a tool that can be used to challenge the departments and groups of the organization to continuously find new improvements and achieve better results. The tool referred to is well-defined targets for each group, and when they exist both management and the groups themselves have the opportunity to continuously raise the bar in order to visualize new improvement potential and avoid boredom. The best way to set targets in the groups is to communicate and break down the company's overall objectives using the catchball method described earlier (see the chapter "Analysis of the Leadership").

The Reality Illusion

We instinctively interpret people's behavior based on our own understanding of the situation where the behavior is observed. But when we relate to each other as if each of us perceived the situation in the same way, we have actually fallen into what authors Steve Zaffron and Dave Logan in their bestselling book *The Three Laws of Performance* refer to as the Reality Illusion. Although there certainly are facts about how things are, the facts of the matter are much less important to us than the way those facts occur to us. There is of course a "real world," but the different positions that well-educated, intelligent people take on a situation are proof of a significant difference between the objective facts of the matter and the way those facts are perceived by the people involved.

Not realizing that people's behavior is a result of how a situation occurs to them creates friction and irritation. For example, if you would address a performance problem without taking your time to understand how the situation occurs to the person performing to your dissatisfaction, the advice you give will probably have very little effect. Why? People won't act differently until they see differently, and trying to change behavior without understanding the other person's perspective is like trying to solve a problem without understanding the root cause. Consequently, if you do not start by seeing the situation from the other person's perspective, your chances of altering that person's behavior are slim. The same goes for the members of a team. If there is no understanding of how reality occurs for each and every person on the team, there will be no common view on reality, and without that most attempts to collaborate will be fruitless.

Where Are You?

Frequent misunderstandings and feelings of disbelief and irritation when observing other people's behavior are the most obvious signs of the Reality Illusion. A team that produces a total effect that is less than the sum of the predicted contribution from each team member is another reason to get suspicious. This is probably a sign of counteracting activities, which are in turn most certainly a result of different views on the purpose of agreed-upon activities and on how they should be performed.

How to Get Out

Getting out of the Reality Illusion starts by realizing that what looks like reality is only how reality occurs to you. If you also realize that with a little effort you can share the same view and vision with others, you are halfway there. There are a number of ways to make sure your team is truly aligned on how to best deliver internal or external customer value. All of them consist in some way of listening to other peoples' views and sharing one's own. The way we used facts to describe our current state and how we used the fishbone to make it easy for everyone to contribute in problem solving at the IT company (see the chapter "The Activities That Started the Improvement Work") are examples of how you can align a team. Some departments also began to conclude their meetings by having everyone responsible for implementing an improvement give a detailed description to his or her colleagues of how he or she was going to perform the task. Some departments even added the columns *why* and *how* to the existing what, who, and when in their to-do lists. This prevented misunderstandings and made sure they had a common view on the purpose and execution of the planned improvements. For sure, all methods where you create a common view on your current and desired states and how the gap between them should be closed are better than other approaches.

Common Ground or Lost in Space?

In 1999, while constructing a Mars orbiter, one team of engineers used the English system of measurement while the rest of their coworkers used the metric system. The use of two different measurement systems made the spacecraft's navigation system malfunction. The small difference in how those involved referred to reality made them lose a satellite worth $125 million in space. This shows that you can save a lot of effort and money by creating common ground.

The Emperor's New Clothes

"The Emperor's New Clothes" is a short tale by the Danish author Hans Christian Andersen about two weavers who promise an emperor a new suit of clothes that is invisible to those unfit for their positions, stupid, or incompetent. When the emperor parades before his subjects in his new clothes, it takes the untainted mind of a child to point out the obvious fact that the emperor is naked.

The pitfall of "The Emperor's New Clothes" could also be called "the We-Are-Not-in-a-Pitfall Pitfall," and it is most common in organizations where a lot of effort and resources have been used to create the "right" structure and to implement the "right" tools and methods. For organizations stuck in this pitfall, seen separately, the improvement process looks flawless. The problem is that it is just that—separate! Improvement is done on the side, and the improvement process therefore runs parallel to the value-creating processes of the organization. Even if the number of implemented improvements is world class and the scores from improvement method self-assessments hit the roof, the performance of the organization remains the same.

Organizations in this pitfall have forgotten the original purpose of what they do and have started doing things for their own sake. They use the right tools but have forgotten why they should be used. On a subconscious level the members of the organization feel that what they do is pointless, but since the unhealthy culture evolved without them noticing, they take comfort in doing what was praised when the improvement initiative was initiated. They continue filling out performance reports, attending meetings, and registering large amounts of improvement activities without any real progress being made. Instead of working with continuous improvement they have fallen into working with continuous change.

Where Are You?

Since there is a lot of activity going on and the improvement process itself looks worthy of imitation this might be the hardest pitfall to spot. The most obvious sign that you are stuck in it is that you have all the tools in place and possibly a high improvement rate as well while indicators regarding customer and employee satisfaction, profitability, and growth have stagnated. Another sign is that improvement activities are done in a mechanistic fashion. Without a link to a higher purpose or a true belief that the activity will make an important difference you won't see any genuine commitment to the activity.

How to Get Out

To get out you need to make the improvement process an integral part of the value-creating processes of your organization. This might sound fancier and more complicated than it is. You start by asking yourselves who you are there to serve both internally and externally. At the IT company we called it our internal and external customers. When you know who your internal and external customers are and what drives their satisfaction, you start questioning what you do. Ask questions such as "Why are we measuring this?" "What is the purpose of this meeting?" "How does this improve our performance?" and "Why do we use this tool?" If you can't give a good answer to the question, stop what you are doing. The saved time can be used for identifying improvements that will make your organization stronger and customers more satisfied.

Are Your Key Performance Indicators Watermelons?

"In my management team we have introduced the concept of Watermelon KPIs. A watermelon is green on the outside and piercing red on the inside, and sometimes our key performance indicators (KPIs) are too," a manager in one of Sweden's largest companies once told me. By becoming aware of the concept of Watermelon KPIs they had become better at confronting the brutal facts of reality and less prone to attempt only to "look good" in front of each other.

The solution could be expressed as turning on the devil's advocate within. In the Middle Ages kings and noblemen had jesters who were employed entertainers with the unique opportunity to—in a humorous and indirect manner—point out the elephant in the room without losing their heads. We are not living in the Middle Ages[Speak up and remember that by questioning purposeless rituals and fruitless initiatives you make it possible to substitute them with valuable improvement work and important strategic initiatives. And even more important, if you do not question them you will foster a degrading culture of window dressing where things will look good on the surface but all energy invested in creating positive change is fruitless.]

The Efficiency Paradox

Walking through workplaces today you might see relics of an old era where work could be defined as monotonous activities that only required mechanical skills. With few exceptions this definition of work has changed. Today most work is complex and variable and requires creativity and flexibility from the people performing the work. With this in mind the number of organizations where these relics are still in use is surprisingly high. What is more, even though many organizations have dismounted their time clocks and done away with their piecework contracts, the basic principle of these methods still characterizes the thinking and behavior of the people working there. In these organizations the general belief is still that the time you spend at work looking busy is what counts. People who are active and look stressed are praised, and people who have nothing to do are given new, sometimes pointless assignments. This way of thinking and behaving creates efficient islands in an ocean of ineffectiveness. There is a lot of stuff going on in each group and department of the organization but the organization as a whole still gets very little done. In this environment, where you focus on keeping all your resources busy, the efficiency of one island creates unnecessary work both for the island itself and for other islands in the ocean.

Where Are You?

If you and your colleagues spend a lot of time storing, sorting, structuring, moving, and searching, you might suspect that you are stuck in the Efficiency Paradox. If you feel uneasy and get a bad conscience when you get some time free for reflection, you can be sure. The urge to keep busy makes people overproduce. The overproduction must be handled by someone—most often the next step in the process—and the handling often consists of the activities mentioned above.

How to Get Out

Start by doing away with any outdated methods for keeping yourself and your colleagues busy and start focusing on creating an efficient flow for customer value creation. The best way to do this is by changing your perspective on efficiency. This is achieved when you shift focus from the efficiency of your resources to the efficiency of your work flows. Resource efficiency shows you how much of the total time the resources that add value within your organization are utilized, whereas flow efficiency is the rate between value-adding time and the total time a unit (for example, a product or a customer) being processed spends in the flow. In order to improve flow efficiency at the IT company, we made sure to not only ask what the internal or external customer wanted but also how much of it they wanted and when they wanted it. We also said that if there was not a need to be satisfied, employees could either help a colleague out satisfying an existing need or take some time to reflect and work with improvements.

And the Winner of the Rat Race Is . . .

. . . a rat! It is important to remember that even if you win the rat race, you are still just a rat. With the mind of a rat you will easily be convinced that you will lose if you stop running. Let the rats run their race, and start using your human brain! When you focus on creating value instead of keeping busy, you will achieve more with a lot less effort. And if you fail doing your thing, your way, you can always take comfort in the fact that you are at least still yourself!

In the end you will of course want to be successful at both satisfying needs and utilizing your resources, that is, achieve both high flow efficiency and high resource efficiency, but if you do not focus on satisfying needs first, your efficient resources won't do you much good. When an organization lets go of its single focus on maximizing the utilization of its resources, the improvement work of that organization can become the growth strategy it is supposed to be.

The Friendship Fallacy

In his seminal work *Flow: The Psychology of Optimal Experience*, Mihaly Csíkszentmihályi outlines the theory that people are happiest when they are in a state of flow—a mental state of operation in which a person performing an activity is fully immersed in a feeling of energized focus, full involvement, and enjoyment in the process of the activity. This is a feeling most people have at times and during which temporal concerns such as time, food, and ego are typically ignored.

For a person to experience flow, the challenge level of the activity and skill level of the person must be in balance. A skillful person who never is challenged will feel bored, and if you challenge a person with a low skill level too much, that person will become anxious. Too big a challenge might even seem like a threat to some people. Threats trigger survival strategies such as fight or flight, and people in general are less uncomfortable among bored people than among people who are fighting or constantly on the defensive. This is the reason why a lot of organizations end up in the Friendship Fallacy. In these organizations, memories of situations where individuals have reacted negatively to a combination of excess outside pressure and an internal feeling of powerlessness make people afraid of asking too much of each other. Instead they tiptoe around one another to avoid ruining the friendly but artificially blithesome atmosphere.

[In the Friendship Fallacy people are rarely called to account and are allowed to be lesser versions of themselves. In organizations stuck here you see waning commitment for and declining effects of the improvement initiative without anybody taking responsibility or being held accountable. Therefore no effective countermeasures are introduced.]

Where Are You?

Since it is a feeling, you might think boredom would be hard to spot. It is not. If your colleagues feel it you probably feel it too, and vice versa. Boredom or, if the situation is even worse, apathy will be in the air if you are stuck in the Friendship Fallacy. When you do get people to attend, the energy level of your improvement meetings will be low, you will have a hard time having people take responsibility for improvement activities, and when they do the likelihood of the tasks being performed according to plan is low.

How to Get Out

If you are a leader who wants to support and coach others in achieving better results by utilizing their full potential, your main job is to help them see and connect with their inner ability. To succeed you yourself need to be able to see their full potential and their strengths. When you are able to do that, the next step to get out of the Friendship Fallacy is a change of method. Most of us are used to stimulating better results using the carrot and stick approach. We raise the bar and use incentives or even threats to get people to perform tasks they don't believe themselves they are able to perform. If we push hard this creates anxiety, and after a few tries we probably give up. The carrot and stick approach taps into people's fear of failure and makes people feel inadequate for not being able to deliver expected results, and that's how you foster the negative and defensive atmosphere called blame culture.

For you as a leader and coach there is a much better alternative. If you start by focusing on the strengths people have, you can tap into their will to succeed. If you and your colleagues look at your current performance level from the perspective of your full potential, you will probably see a gap. By letting employees know that, based on their strengths, you expect more from them, you tap into their desire to fulfill their own potential and get improved business results as a by-product.

At the IT company the groups or individuals being coached had always taken part in developing their own targets. When there was an intrinsic drive to achieve targets, a belief in people's ability, and available support if anyone should encounter difficulties, an environment where we could challenge each other in a new way was created. Being challenged this way might be tough too, but it is often something completely different and much better than people are used to. It might even open their eyes to the extent of their capacity, and if that happens a huge creative power will be unleashed.

Let's All Slip into Something More Uncomfortable!

"Being a leader at this plant demands a lot of courage. On our continuous improvement journey we address people's desire to utilize their full potential. At times we are all afraid of not living up to the expectations of the surrounding world, but if we give in to that fear our behavior becomes controlling and inhibiting," a managing director at a very profitable Fortune 100 company once told me. "By stretching our own comfort zone as managers, we maintain a safe environment where others can stretch theirs, and that is when we all grow," she continued.

The turning point at the IT company was when we went from finger-pointing to taking responsibility and ownership. When managers started taking responsibility for the development of their colleagues and stepped into their shoes as owners of the performance of their departments instead of blaming the incompetence of their subordinates, results improved. And even more important, relationships between people went from very superficial friendships to deep and mutual trust.

Epilogue

Since my dinner with Roger, I have helped dozens of organizations around the world, both manufacturing and service organizations, to achieve long-term improvement in performance by supporting the development of a high-performance improvement culture. While working with these organizations I have time and time again been struck by the power of the basic principles for successful improvement work we used at the IT company. Combined with the knowledge of the five cultural pitfalls, they drastically improve an organization's chances of succeeding with continuous improvement!

I wish you all the best on your continuous improvement journey!

Additional Reading

Creating, Robert Fritz, Fawcett Columbine, 1991.

Flow: The Psychology of Optimal Experience, Mihály Csíkszentmihályi, Harper & Row, 1990.

Getting the Right Things Done, Pascal Dennis, The Lean Enterprise Institute, 2006.

Good to Great: Why Some Companies Make the Leap . . . and Others Don't, Jim Collins, BookHouse Editions, 2001.

The High-Velocity Edge: How Market Leaders Leverage Operational Excellence to Beat the Competition, Steven J. Spear, McGraw-Hill Professional, 2010.

Ideas Are Free: How the Idea Revolution Is Liberating People and Transforming Organizations, Alan G. Robinson and Dean M. Schroeder, Berrett-Koehler Publishers, 2004.

Influencer: The Power to Change Anything, Kerry Patterson, Joseph Grenny, David Maxfield, Ron MacMillan, and Al Switzler, McGraw-Hill, 2007.

Lean Production Simplified, Pascal Dennis, Productivity Press, 2002.

Make Things Happen, Lars Nilsson, C2 Management AB, 1997.

The Other Side of the Card: Where Your Authentic Leadership Story Begins, Mike Morrison, McGraw-Hill, 2007.

Profit Beyond Measure: Extraordinary Results Through Attention to Work and People, H. Thomas Johnson and Anders Bröms, Free Press, 2008.

The 7 Habits of Highly Effective People, Stephen R. Covey, Free Press, 2004.

Your Own Reflections and Improvements

About the Author

Joakim Ahlström is Sweden's leading authority on creating a continuous improvement culture. Joakim is a popular inspirational speaker and an appreciated business coach who has helped many companies across the globe, both manufacturing and service organizations, to achieve long-term improvement in performance by supporting the development of a high-performance continuous improvement culture. In Sweden, *How to Succeed with Continuous Improvement* is one of the most read books on continuous improvement.